To Ellie

John Edward Radcliffe

Storms of the Scottish Isles

*Dark tales of creatures and beings
on the remote islands of the North Atlantic*

JOHN EDWARD RADCLIFFE

All stories in this book are fantasy and while some contain reference to actual events and places, those particular events and places have been altered to fit the story line.

AUTHOR'S NOTE

There is an archipelago where Chance has provided an eclectic combination of scenery, objects, peoples and mythology. Mountains rise high directly from the sea. Huge cliffs, navigable caves, sea-carved monoliths, skerries, and over five hundred islands dot the ocean. Ancient tombs, brochs, duns, huge standing stones and circles, cairns, and Stone Age settlements too numerous to count cover these islands like salt on pretzels. Black houses, castles, churches and cathedrals, mills, crofts, and distilleries give evidence of clans, communities and crafts of more recent times. Water kelpies, nuggles, sheen, fisher-folk, selkies, and trows join the usual collection of faerie folk in island mythology. Scots English, Gaelic and Old Norse are all still living languages, and each inhabited island has its own community, history, and identity. Sun, wind, storm, warm and cold, mist and clear, can all occur within one day, and each resonates with the landscape.

Hundreds of these isles stretch from the Sea of the Hebrides, through the North Sea and into the Norwegian Sea, some of the most violent waters in the world. These are remote lands, sparsely inhabited, somewhat difficult to traverse, often wet and boggy, with few trees and surrounded by open sea.

All of these things impact the imagination, but asked to pick one, I would pick the storms. Think of the roar of the unimpeded wind, the driving rain flooding the one lane roadways, the clouds enshrouding the peaks, the lightning flashing around the ancient monuments, the waves smashing on the cliffs, and the people in oilskins and boots who must tend the sheep or fish the sea, struggling against the blow.

John Edward Radcliffe
27 August 2008

TABLE OF CONTENTS

INTRODUCTION

Big Murdock MacLean and his wife Mary Martin of Killmuir, Skye, brought their four children including Angus, named for Mary's brother, to Point Prim on Prince Edward Island in 1805. Murdock was 50 years old. He was indentured to Lord Sinclair. (Murdock's father was Alan Maclean who is related to the MacLaines of Lochbuie on the Isle of Mull.)

The family finally purchased a farm on Point Prim which eventually Angus farmed. Angus married Mary Murchison, also from Point Prim. They, in turn, had six boys and four girls.

Samuel, the youngest of the brood, married Kate Warmington, and they and their family moved from PEI to Wollaston, a suburb of Quincy, Massachusetts. By heritage, Scottish men were fishermen, shipbuilders or quarry men. Quincy granite was prized for its fine grain and shipped world-wide as building material. Quincy's Fore River Shipyard was one of the largest in the United States.

Samuel and Kate had three boys and six girls. One of their sons, James, was my grandfather. He married Mary Stewart, and they had seven children. My mother, Florence Catharine MacLean, was the second child. As the oldest girl, she helped raise the follow-on children and didn't marry until she was in her late twenties.

The MacLean families were all large, and, until they moved from PEI, the children continued to marry other Scots. In my mother's time they were still thoroughly Scottish, people of the isles. For one thing they had the old Scottish superstitions. If a spoon would fall to the floor, salt spill, or a mirror break, there were rituals involved for expiation. If a guest were to arrive and tea be offered, he or she would have to wait for the hot water. The kettle was always full sitting on the back burner so the water was warm but not boiling. My MacLean mother would then dump the warm water down the sink and refill the kettle with cold water from the faucet. She would put this on the front burner to eventually get it hot enough to boil and make tea. When asked why she didn't just put the already warm water on the front burner, she would answer that everyone knows that cold water heats faster than warm.

There was a witch in the family. At a time when witchcraft was considered lunacy, not a vocation, it was still esteemed by the Quincy MacLean family. Tina, one of my grandmother Mary's sisters, was held in awe by Mary's children. Now the next generation, mine, held her in fear.

So before we travel to the islands for our stories, I'd like to introduce you to my Scottish family and at least one story, and there are many, of the MacLeans of Quincy.

Hill Top House

Tina was a witch, a real witch

The Ideal wood stove was an ingenious device that could be assembled without tools. The cast iron base looked like a serving platter with a slot in each corner for the tab of a cast, claw-shaped foot. The weight of the base held the feet in position without the use of screws or bolts. The same was true of the four cast iron sides of the stove which had tabs along each edge. Those along the bottom edge fit into holes in the cast iron base, along their sides into the end plates, and finally on the top into the cast iron cooking surface. In addition, the cooking surface plate had large round holes filled with round covers. When someone desired direct heat, such as when frying, one of the round covers could be removed to allow the flame to touch the bottom of the cooking pan. The round cover to the left front of the top plate contained a series of concentric rings that lifted separately so that smaller pans could be accommodated.

Because all of the parts were "as cast," they did not fit tight. Cracks between the plates supplied air to the fire but allowed errant flames to escape into the room. For that reason the stove was located some distance from the wall and mounted on a metal sheet which, in turn, had an asbestos pad under it to keep the heat from igniting the wooden floor.

At one end of the stove was a hinged, side door for charging the fire box. A second and larger door was hinged on the front plate to give access to the oven.

The Ideal stove was located in the kitchen of Hill Top House.

Actually my story should have started in the Scottish Isles. Mull, Iona, Coll, Tiree, a snippet of Skye and a chunk of the main land were all MacLean Clan property. When you lived on clan lands, you took the clan name so the sheer size of the land holdings assured a large number of MacLeans. The MacLeans were Jacobites. Following the defeat of Prince Charlie's forces at Culloden their land holdings were forfeited to the Crown, and eventually the clansmen and their families were scattered to the winds. Murdock MacLean sailed from Skye on the *Polly* in 1805 to a new home on Prince Edward Island. After working off his indenture, with the help of Lord Selkirk, he purchased a farm on Point Prim. A century later Samuel MacLean, his wife Kate, and children left PEI and moved to Quincy, Massachusetts, attracted by the granite quarries and the Scottish trade of stone cutting.

His son James and his wife Mary Stewart had seven children and those children, in turn, twenty grandchildren. I am one of those grandchildren, the son of Florence MacLean who was the second of James' children. When I was growing up, every Sunday the whole Quincy family would gather for dinner at my grandparents' house. We were a typical Scottish family with the exception of Tina. She was a witch.

Tina was sister to my Grandmother Mary. She had grown somewhat overweight but could still exhibit the aggressiveness and great strength typical of Scottish women. The adults agreed that, "Tina loves children." I can assure you that the feeling was not mutual. We were afraid of Tina.

In the winter Tina lived in the spacious attic of my grandparents' house. In the summer she rented a large bungalow on a hill in Bristol, New Hampshire. The grandchildren were invited to stay with her, and the adults promoted it. The MacLean families were proud but poor so vacations were hard to finance. Sending your children to stay with Tina at

Hill Top House was like sending them to summer camp, a very inexpensive summer camp. Now, I don't want you to think they sent us off alone with no one but spooky Tina to watch over us. At least one of the parents would stay with us, rotating each week or two. They weren't completely blind to Tina's eccentricities.

Our distaste for Tina was offset by the pleasure we got from each other's companionship. We grandchildren were all great friends. Then, too, there was the location of the House. The Newfound River flowed by the bottom of the hill with a fine swimming hole just a quarter mile down river. Newfound Lake itself was less than three miles away with swimming, sunning, and fishing. We even had friends among the locals but kept them far away from Tina. We knew she would scare them off.

There was a pattern to life at Hill Top House. Each morning, seven days a week, we would meet in the kitchen to wait for our turn in the outhouse. Tina would have a large pot boiling on the Ideal, and the room would be lit by a strange combination of the early sun and the flickering bursts of flame through the plate separations of the stove. The curls of flame and the heat radiating from the stove made the room seem like the cone of a volcano. With the addition of the steam from the pot, the room was a virtual sauna.

Tina would wait until her audience was gathered and then lift the caldron from the stove and hustle it through the back door out onto the rock patio. Then she would splash the hot water first this way and then that to scald the snakes she said were waiting for the unfortunate outhouse visitor that couldn't wait for her to clear the path. Every third or forth splash would be accompanied by "gotchya" to convince us of her success. Was she pulling our chains? You bet she was. We danced up and down, waiting our turn, and Tina enjoyed every minute of our discomfort.

As we made our morning call, Tina laid out basins of hot water on the patio for our scrub up before breakfast. There were no baths, but even Tina went to the river for a cleansing swim.

Breakfast was always the same, hot oatmeal with milk, one egg and toast singed over the flame which licked through an open cover hole of the Ideal. Right after breakfast we each made a bag lunch including a warm soda. We would cool the soda in the river while we swam. On rainy days, and there were a few, we would play board games in the living room, and if it was a Saturday, we would be taken to town for the matinee at the movies. On the days when we went to the lake, the parent of the week would walk over and back with us. Most of us were early teenagers, and the platoon system was always in force. We had to be back at the house for supper chores. I knew that most of the chores were "make work," but it felt good to be a part of our only team effort. After supper it was radio time or some Tina show. Her show was always spooky with fortune reading, tables rising or spirits speaking. Just the thing we needed to create nightmares.

By nine o'clock at night we were all in bed, exhausted from the day's exercise. We fell asleep almost as our heads hit the pillows. Our parent of the week would be in bed by eleven, and all should have been quiet until morning. Yet, at midnight all the children would be awake waiting for a continuation of the horror show. Tina, candle in hand, would walk past the bedroom door, cackling and mumbling. After several passes all would be quiet until morning.

On Sunday we would go to the village church. It said Methodist on the sign so the Presbyterians among us enjoyed the catholicity while the Roman Catholics and the Episcopalians were enlightened by the Protestant austerity. After church we would stay around the house until the mid-afternoon meal, change into old clothes and visit Morton's farm a mile down the road. Morton's wife Flora was a distant relative of the MacLean's. Tina drove Morton and Flora crazy, but they enjoyed the children because they had none of their own.

The last year Tina rented Hill Top House, age having taken its toll, was ended on a rather sour note. Each morning's wait for our trip to the outhouse and each nighttime's midnight terror drove our group closer together until in late summer we united under the battle cry, "Get the witch." It was a silent cry for none of us dared to cross her. Who wanted to spend the rest of his or her life as a toad? Then a plan emerged. We decided to play her game. The first chance was early in the afternoon. Tina was locked in the outhouse reading the paper. Francis and I ran up on the stoop just outside the locked door. "Did you see that snake?" he exclaimed.

"Where did he go?" I asked.

"Under the outhouse," Francis answered.

"Maybe he'll climb up from the pit through the seat hole inside?"

Fran jiggled the latch. "The door is locked. We'll have to let him go. What a shame!"

Then we walked off and left Tina to face the slithering apparition.

We spent the rest of the afternoon real snake hunting and captured a small one in a large jar. Lack of oxygen made it languid so we placed it on Tina's chair at supper. As it turned out, she sat without looking, jumped to her feet and screamed as the half-squashed reptile slithered away. The rest of the evening we took turns walking about the house, cackling and mumbling, mimicking Tina. When it was time to go up to bed, we lined up to visit the outhouse but refused to go until Tina chased the snakes away. It was all great fun. Tina couldn't punish us all.

In forcing Tina to heat water to scald the snakes so late in that evening, we led her to stoke the stove to an extraordinary level so that it was still gaining heat as we prepared for bed. The area of the stove's exhaust was becoming cherry red, and the exhaust pipe was beginning to smoke. "Look at that!" cried Francis. "The whole stove will be red soon." I feared he was right.

I smelled a wisp of smoke as I prepared for bed. Chimney smoke recirculation, I reassured myself.

At midnight I awoke to find our attic bedroom filled with smoke. The house was on fire! The crazy witch! I was sure she had set the place on fire just to pay us back. I went to wake the parent of the week, Nan, who was sleeping in the room across the hall. She was already awake and pulling on a robe. Nan and I ran down the hall to the stairway only to find flames at the bottom of the staircase. We were trapped. I returned to the boys' bedroom to wake the others while Nan got the girls up.

Across the hall I heard coughing, and Lorna came out of the room, tears streaming down her cheeks. Before I could stop her, she ran to the stairs only to return screaming.

The smoke was increasing, and Maureen and Francis, still full of sleep came out to join us. "The house is on fire," Lorna told them. "We can't get out!"

It all seemed to be happening so fast. I could see smoke coming through the cracks in the floor boards. Nan herded us into the girl's bedroom. It had a window in a gable facing out onto the roof.

The window had four lights and was made with heavy wooden cross pieces. We pushed and pulled, but it would not open. "Find a chamber pot, a stool, a chair, anything heavy to knock out the window," Nan urged. With the children coughing and wailing, the smoke swirling, and the floor boards warming, panic replaced reason. We bumped around, finding nothing and tumbling over each other causing even more panic.

The girls were screaming. Fear had overtaken reason. Francis had dropped to his knees and was gasping for breath. There were tears running down his cheeks. I could see the flicker of flames in the hall.

I was the oldest of the children and somehow thought that I was expected to take the leadership role. But what could I do? I couldn't kick the window out. I was in my bare feet. No less panicked than the rest, I made a bad choice and attacked the window with my fore arm. Nan grabbed me just in time for I would surely have sliced it through to the bone. She pushed me backwards until I stumbled to the floor.

To my shock she kneeled beside me on the floor and began to shake me. "John, John, wake up. You will miss breakfast."

I could see her looking down at me. I was in bed. The smoke was gone. It had been a nightmare.

I got out of bed in my pajamas and followed Nan down the stairs. The others had already been out to the outhouse. Everyone was quiet except for Tina who seemed to be in a very jolly mood. One might have chocked that up to the fact that we were leaving that very morning to return home. Or was it something else?

I couldn't bring myself to tell the others of my dream. They would all laugh at me. In fact, I told no one, not even my parents although the impact of the dream took weeks to wear off. Time and again I would wake up to the smell of smoke and lose the rest of my night's sleep. Tina's revenge? Why me? We all bugged her. I think even Nan was a part of the teasing for she must have known that we were purposely irritating Tina.

Decades passed, and Nan, 85 and a chain smoker, finally succumbed to blocked carotid arteries. She went in and out of a coma. I flew out to the coast knowing that it was only a matter of days until she died. Landing at Logan Airport, I rented a car and drove to South Shore Hospital. Nan seemed asleep, but then, suddenly waking to one of her brief, lucid moments she beckoned me to her bedside and spoke softly into my ear, "Do you remember the night Hill Top House burned?" I wasn't the only dreamer. Tina had taken revenge on all of us.

Then there were the family recollections of their Scottish homeland.

At this point there is some confusion because the stories my mother was told by her father relate to the MacLeans of Duart. Intermarriage muddies the clan tree, but research links us to the MacLaines of Lochbuie. Both clans had castles on the Isle of Mull.

"We were pirates," my mother would tell me. "We would watch from the castle for ships coming thru the inner waterway and sail out and board them. Then we would exact a toll for their safe passage." This definitely refers to the MacLeans of Duart.

There was intermarriage between the clan branches on the island of Mull. MacLaines of Lockbuie married MacLeans of Duart so who is to say who is who? It was the stories of Duart piracy and pictures of Duart Castle that lead me to the isles in the first place.

So I traveled to the islands, and using imagination and the lore of the isle folk, created stories to fit the travels. Admittedly there are stories everywhere. But I knew long before I made the first trip that these isles and their people were a special lot. My family was special. All of the qualities of the tales are embodied in the people, even those like mine that had left the isles two hundred years ago.

The stories are not in chronological order but rather by region to represent the pattern of travel. They were originally a polyglot of stories I told to Boy Scouts, schools, story telling groups, friends, my children, grandchildren and at festivals and special events.

CHAPTER ONE

SKYE

DUNVEGAN

SLIGACHAN
CUILLINS
LOCH
CORUISK

ELGOL

Imagination is a free gift given us by the loving Father of us all. Stimulated by experience, it can be a tool to enhance our lives, to create a separate and very different existence, an escape from the ordinary.

The misty isles stretch all the way from Ailsa Craig in the Firth of Clyde to the most northern Shetland isle of Unst in the Norwegian Sea. In total, these dots of rock, earth and peat number over five hundred. Some are no more than rocks or skerries while others in clusters are more like small states with their own history and language. The isles enjoy an unusually warm and moist climate due to the flow of the Gulf Stream diverted by Cape Cod across the Atlantic into their path. These northern isles experience the long, dark days of winter and the midnight sun of summer just as their Norwegian neighbors do, but not the intense cold nor the summer's heat. The surrounding sea tempers the extremes.

The isles have been occupied since the Stone Age and have no end of well-preserved artifacts including tombs, standing stones and the cave dwellings of these ancients. Even to this day many of these ruins have not been excavated.

The islands can be classified into three main groups with a few stragglers: the Western Isles or Hebrides, the Orkneys and the Shetlands. The Hebrides have been a part of Scotland since the birth of the nation at the crowning of Kenneth MacAlpin around 850 AD. The Orkneys and the Shetlands were annexed from Norway in 1470 AD as payment of the dowry of Princess Ann. However, the Scottish presence in these islands predates the transfer by hundreds of years since the church orders were tied to the Scottish abbeys, and Scottish saints converted the settlers.

At the time of my earliest travels fifty years ago, the language of the Hebrides was Scots/English and Gaelic while the far northern isles of the Shetlands were Scots/English and Old Norse. Electricity was just coming to the rural parts of the isles, and TV was a curiosity. Tourism was, for the most part, still restricted to the larger and more southern Isles.

If you have only one island to see, which would it be? My choice would be the Isle of Skye. In the days of my earliest travels, there was no bridge connecting it to the mainland as there is now. Skye's claim to fame was as a remote climbing center with the Red and Black Cuillins challenging the best of mountaineers.

The island had a long and bloody history. It was a land fought over for centuries by the MacDonald's and the Macleod's. Fortress and castle ruins attest to the fierceness of the battles.

It contains marvelous mountain scenery, lakes, waterfalls, stone formations, multiple castles and great houses, and spectacular sunsets. It is the land of the Sheen, the fairies, the people of the hills.

Just think of the wonderful stories you could imagine there.

The Bell Ringer

When it rains, it pours

When you look back nearly fifty years, you tend to remember things through your filter of understanding. Your mind tries to make sense of those things that made little or no sense at the time.

The howling of force six winds and the pounding of torrential rain led to the frustration of waiting days for a chance to climb in the surrounding Cuillins. I was wasting away, trapped in the climber's hotel in Sligachan in the middle of nowhere on the Isle of Skye. It could have driven me mad. That would explain the weekend's events.

I stood in the face of the gale on the ancient stone bridge in front of the hotel. Rain poured down my poncho and beat on the seal skin wrap of the small, old lady at my side. Now I say old, but that is in terms of my youth at the time. Actually she must have been middle-aged. I was in a rage. The storm was robbing me. It was thwarting my great passion for climbing.

The small woman's presence finally dawned on me. Where the devil had she come from, and why was she standing here? I didn't see her come. To hell with her. I had my own problems. I'd leave this island tomorrow morning. Waiting out the rain was hopeless.

"Don't go without seeing the island," she said, holding a hand in front of her mouth as she talked to keep out the wind-driven torrent. "Are you a climber? Do you climb unaided?"

"Yes and yes, if I could get the chance." Then, responding to her sightseeing appeal, "What sense is there touring this soggy, storm-soaked chunk of rock? No one in his right mind would be fool enough to drive these roads in this weather." I found I was yelling just to be heard over the roar of the wind.

"You climb unaided because you want adventure. Think of driving the coast roads in this storm, with the breakers blowing in from the sea, and torrents of runoff pouring out from roadside embankments. Rivers and waterfalls will be gushing, swollen from the runoff. Villages will be buttoned down while pubs and shops stand as isolated islands of commerce in the desolation. It would be a thrill. From here you can drive the Glen Drynock Road. It will take you along the coast all the way to Dunvegan. You can't leave Skye without seeing Dunvegan," she implored.

I felt a compulsion, a sudden yearning to see the island. I was losing my mind! "Let's get inside before we drown!" My words were lost. She was gone.

Hanging my wet clothes over the radiator in my room, I sat and ruminated. It would be an adventure I thought.

Dinner in the common room was my one pleasure. I could air my complaints with the other climbers. We could commiserate together. But that night they were missing. They probably gave up and went on their way. In their place was a group obviously from the surrounding countryside, apparently taking a break from the tedious isolation of the stormy weather. At the table across from me were what appeared in the dim light to be twins dressed in overalls and wool shirts. They were dressed a bit warm for the room. To my left in a booth was a couple that could have been Jack Sprat and his wife. She was short and hefty while he was a bean pole. She was full of laughter and seemed to be responding to lively conversation. At another table further to my left sat an ancient couple, who were arguing over a spill of beer that was dripping off the edge of their table. Then the twins grew animated, and one pointed at me. I was not imagining it; they were discussing me. As I turned in their direction, and before I could ask them what was going on, I heard a movement. Someone was pulling up a chair on my right to join me at my table. "Do you mind if I eat with you?" the priest asked. "I'm Father Zack."

"No, of course not. That is an unusual name. I'm John. Are you staying here?" leaving off my last name since it is English.

"I saw you talking to the Rain Maiden. Are you going to take her advice? This is the Holy weekend, you know. I hope you will stay and join us at the sunrise. In any case you will have to try the special tonight, lamb stew." Each of the three items he brought up could have been fodder for conversation. Rain Maiden? Holy weekend? Stew? Yet, after bringing up this jumble of confusion, he seemed quite content to simply sit and wait for the waitress.

We both ordered the lamb. The so-called Rain Maiden was forgotten. The meal was spent discussing the spread of electricity and telephones to the villages in the coming year and the changes that would make. He then noted that the people around us were here for their one big meal before they began the strict fast which would last until the sunrise, Sunday morning. I told him that the way things were going the sun wasn't likely to rise any time soon.

"What part of the island do you come from, Father?"

As he noted the location, it became clear that his village was one I would pass through if I drove towards Dunvegan the next morning. He offered to show me around. "Just stop in at the rectory at any time during the day."

I agreed to his offer with the one codicil; I had not yet decided what to do. I was strongly tempted to leave the island and drive south out of the dreary weather.

As the twins were leaving, they stopped to say, "We look forward to seeing you."

Seeing me, I thought? Look forward? Why did they think I'd see them?

I slept like a rock that night while the wind howled and the rain pounded on the windows. Nothing bothered me. I had made up my mind. I was off on another adventure. I had decided to tour the island. It would be a wild ride.

Early the next morning I headed west up the Glen Drynoch Road, and the mountains shielded me from the fierce storm. The road forked at the village of Drynock. Eight miles later it was joined by the road from Portree. After I passed Barcadale, the next small village, the road skirted the shore. My protection was gone, and the car shuddered from wind bursts. That same wind drove salt spray across the windshield making it hard to see the road ahead. Coming down a ridge I suddenly realized that there were sheep in the road. I panicked and jammed on the brakes, skidding into the ditch at the roadside. My head struck the wheel, and for a moment I was stunned.

"Can you get out?" It was a young girl banging on my window. "Get out and come with me. There is a garage up the hill."

I pulled on my poncho and noted blood on my hands from a cut on my forehead. "I can make it," I said, climbing out the door and starting up the road. "You go home and get out of the downpour. I'll be fine." We were both yelling to be heard over the storm.

"I'll go with you."

"No need, I'm OK. How far?" As I looked at her standing there, I had a feeling I had met her mother at the stone bridge. Perhaps it was her seal skin poncho that created the resemblance. "You need to get out of this wet. I'll be fine."

"I can't leave you. The bell ringer is my charge." She led the way up the road to a small stone garage. I could not see electric service and shuddered at the primitive nature of the facility. What chance did I have here? Cold and soaked, I could at least hope they had a peat fire inside. The sign said "James Brothers, Mechanics."

A man came to the door to let us into the office. "Are you Mr. James?" He just stood and stared.

"James MacCann," he finally said.

"James MacCann," came an echo from the garage proper.

"My father..." He was interrupted.

"Our father promised to name the first-born boy James," said the twin entering from the garage. The twins from last night at the inn, I thought. "But he couldn't tell us apart."

"Don't let it distract you," said the young girl realizing that my car was not the only thing getting mired down.

Trying to overlook the confusion, I addressed my problem. "My car is off the road back down the hill."

"I'll get my horse."

And, said the echo, "I'll get my horse."

"Is that one or two horses?" I asked.

"A little slow even for a tourist," said James one.

"Be kind. You can see he hit his head," said James two.

While they hitched the team of two horses, I turned my attention to the girl. "What is your name?"

"Nediam. Nediam Niar."

Russian? Polish? Perhaps Slavic. "Nediam, don't they have a tow truck here?"

In ten minutes they had the car back at the garage, but it would not start. "Probably just wet. Unfortunately, it is the Holy Weekend, and we can do no work. We will work on it first thing Monday morning."

"By rights we should have left the car in the ditch."

"I remembered the lost sheep on the Sabbath so my conscious is clear," said James one.

"But I was the Good Samaritan," said James two.

"That wasn't on a holy day."

"How do you know? Were you there?"

We left them arguing.

I followed Nediam down a path to a side road and then to the door of a stone house set on the slope of the hill overlooking the village. The sign over the door said, "Doctor Johnston."

"They will take you in," assured Nediam.

The door opened, and a short, stocky woman stood there blocking the doorway. "We call her Four by Four." I was embarrassed by Nediam's remark. Obviously, the woman could hear it, but she didn't pay heed. She looked right past Nediam as though she were not there.

The isles people are generous and welcoming, and this fine woman was case in point. She saw that we were drenched to the skin and immediately ushered us in. Before saying a word she guided us to the living room and the warm peat fire. Then she said, "My name is Louise, but you can call me Four, short for Four by Four." Remembering her as one of the odd couple I had labeled Jack Sprat and his wife from the dinner at the inn, I wondered what I would be told to call her husband, the skinny doctor.

I told her about the accident and the need to find a place to stay the weekend.

"We are a guest house, and since we have no guests at this time of the year, you can have your pick of rooms. I'll set up a rack so you can hang your clothes by the fire. Today and tomorrow are fast days so we all have to starve a bit, but I can bring you hot tea."

"That will be fine." I looked to see what had happened to Nediam, but she had slipped away.

"My husband is the village doctor so he is out on calls. The rain brings out all kinds of illness. This has been a particularly severe storm. A little more rain falls, and some of the houses will collapse, undermined by the runoff. The main brook that supplies the village water has gone mad, and all our tap water is muddy. I wouldn't plan on taking a bath."

The door opened again, and a rain-soaked man entered. "Wants me to bleed her. Can you believe that?" The doctor was arriving home.

"Miss Wilkins, I imagine," said Four.

"That woman and her bad fluxes drive me crazy. And she ends up telling me what she wants me to do. Might as well be her own doctor. Hello, I'm Jack."

"Really? Jack?" I was so bemused I could not make a sensible reply. "Oh, I'm John."

"Are you staying the weekend?" Then, realizing he had bluntly broken in on his wife's inn keeping he apologetically noted, "My day off tomorrow. We'll see Dunvegan." It seemed that everyone wanted to be my tour guide.

I changed into bed clothes, for it was late in the day. In the spring the sun is still shining in the evening this far north so the dark clouds were a God-send. I hung my wet clothes on a stand Four placed in front of the hearth. She served tea piping hot in the kitchen, and we sat around the table, Four, Jack, and I, getting acquainted. After perhaps a pleasant hour, I excused myself and retired upstairs to the room I had selected.

The room was clean and neat and the bed ideal for rest. I laid out dry clothes for the morning and within minutes fell deeply into a dream-less sleep.

Early the next morning we were seated in Jack's Austin and off to the ancestral home of the MacLeods, Castle Dunvegan. Somehow Nediam had gotten into the back seat but just sat and watched the two of us. Doctor Jack paid no attention to her, and she didn't seem to mind.

Four had packed several scones and a thermos of tea, a poor fare but generous in light of the fast. "The castle will be closed, but we will see the grounds and especially the seals. That oilskin will keep you dry. It's basic uniform for the fishermen. Did I tell you about the Fairy Flag that hangs inside the castle? It is a fake. Supposed to have saved the MacLeods in battle twice and be good for one more time. Actually, it's an old bar towel. But not just any bar towel. It's the one they used to wipe the bar after Queen Vicky visited. It was Vicky that brought us chimneys you know. Used to use holes in the roof. The underside of the roof would get so coated with soot that it would rain down in a storm coloring everyone and everything in the house black."

We were soon down the path beside the castle that led to the shore. "Try to step on the bigger stones. They won't be as likely to turn under your foot." Nediam helped me negotiate the wet and slippery shore. She was like a mother keeping her child out of trouble. Nothing was to happen to her bell ringer.

The seals were basking on a large rock in the harbor. I could swear that several lifted their flippers in a wave to us. "May be a selkie among them you know," said Jack. The castle rose behind us looking dark and ominous with the storm clouds as the backdrop.

As I expected, the scones were not enough, and we all returned to the guest house starved. Porridge was to be the fare for the evening, but Chance interfered. "You need to see the back yard, Jack. It is a lake and will soon push this stone house down the hill!" Four was obviously worried, and as we looked out the back window, it became clear that her worry was understated. Run-off from the hill had created a swimming pool-like pond trapped by the stone house and the walled yard.

The doctor was a man of action. "Shut the doors on the hall." We jumped to his command. "Now open the front door wide and block it." Next, he pushed open the back door, and the torrent of water flowed through the house like a sluice, out the front door and down the front steps into the street. The initial flow was huge, but as time went on the river became a stream and then a brook and finally a tiny creek. As the flood subsided, it left three huge fish on the front doorstep.

"Louise, get the Reverend Zack. We have a miracle to display."

Just moments later she returned with Father Zack who didn't seem a bit surprised to see me there. He declared that the fish had been delivered by the Holy Sprit, and no one else, and that it would be unwise to overlook the gift. In spite of the fast, we must force ourselves to eat the fish, and he, Father Zack, would help. "Surely, this man is a saint," we said as we stuffed our empty stomachs. Only Nediam failed to eat.

We had just finished when we heard a cry for help. It was distant and would have been missed if the front door had been closed.

A path led from the road in front of the house to the bay. There it intersected the bay roadway. To our left a sand beach appeared to stretch the entire length of the bay. To our right was a short stub of land with a beacon at the end. At the foot of the stub, they were dragging someone out of the surf. Doctor Jack rushed to the man's side while a woman pushed her way through the small crowd to ask, "Archie, what were you doing in there? Tuesday is bath day." At that exact moment a very selective, huge gust of wind caught her, and as though pulled by some giant hand, she went caroming down the beach and into the surf. For a moment the old man was left alone as all now turned to help drag her out of the water. An especially fearsome wave, accompanied by a gust that must have been force eight, then washed the whole party into the surf. Even the doctor was carried in. It took a good half hour to sort it all out and complete a nose count to be sure no one was lost.

Nediam explained to me that Archie was a heavy drinker. It was his job to light the bay light at dusk, and somewhat intoxicated, he had fallen into the water. Luckily, he had managed to be washed ashore rather than out into the ocean.

When I looked at the two of them, Archie and his wife, dripping wet on the shore, I realized that they had been the old man and lady with the spilled beer at the dinner at Sligachan.

As we all walked back up the beach, the cry for help came again. Archie had tried to light the beacon a second time and, as before, had fallen in. Half-drowned the town folk had to turn back and drag him out again. Once on shore, Four by Four grabbed him by the collar and dragged him out to the beacon where his coal lantern stood and lit the light herself. Then she pulled and shoved him back safely to the roadway. "It is lit, Archie. Now, go home and dry out." The several dozen soaked villagers did the same.

"Fourth time this month," said Nediam.

"Why not retire him?"

"Then what would everyone do for excitement?"

The doctor was busy all evening seeing patients with pneumonia, flu and common colds, abetted by the weather.

"The storm will end tomorrow morning," said Four. What makes tomorrow so special, I thought?

Nediam went home, and I went upstairs to change my clothes. I had to trudge through the stream in the lower hall so I left my shoes on the stairs. No sense tracking the wet into the bedroom. If anything, the storm seemed to get worse that night. How could they expect it to end in the morning?

We were all up before my usual rising time for we had bedded down early. Early bedtimes and mornings were a natural thing in a society without electricity. Dressed for the weather, we walked, or should I say sloshed, our way up the hill at the end of the village to the churchyard overlooking the bay. The whole village was there. In the rain the villagers were dark shapes wavering in this and that direction driven by the wind. The rain was light but persistent. The villagers were gathered and waiting patiently. Nediam explained, "They are waiting for the bell." Time passed slowly in the storm. Not even the best oilskin could keep one dry in this kind of weather.

Finally, in frustration I asked, "What is taking it so long?"

Nediam said, "Go; see." She pointed to the church. I turned, pressed through the crowd, and walked to the church. As I entered the narthex, there stood Archie, the bell rope in a pile at his feet.

"It came off. Now the sun won't come. We will miss our chance." He kicked at the rope in anger.

"Where was it attached?"

"On that arm." He pointed up the tower. The arm was more than three stories above us. I looked for the ladder rungs. There weren't any.

The wind howled as it passed through the belfry. The storm continued to ravage the village folk standing outside.

I suddenly realized that I had been recruited. Of course! I was a mountain climber. I grabbed one end of the rope and tucked it in my belt, jumped and swung up onto the first beam. The next beam was overhead but crossed this one about eight feet above it. The only way to get to it was to edge out on this beam and, at the center, jump for the one above. The wind was blowing rain in the windows of the belfry. The beam was wet and slippery. "It won't go," my common sense old me, and, in the past, I had trusted that voice.

The stone wall of the tower sloped in so climbing the wall without tools was out of the question. Then I saw that Nediam was sitting on the far side of the tower on my beam! "Who is the climber here?" I asked.

"Pointing she said, "Use the rungs," and I saw them on the wall, a good six feet away. They had been hidden in the shadows of the dull light. Would they hold? If not I'd fall only eight feet. No big deal so I jumped for them and landed cleanly like a spider. The rungs were wet and rusty but otherwise solid. I climbed to the second beam. The rungs ended at this beam. The arm was above by another ten feet and on the other side of the tower.

The wind in the tower grew stronger as you went higher, nearer the windows. The rain was blurring my eyesight. There sat Nediam on the second beam! I had worked to get there, and she had obviously used some shortcut to join me. "If you can do that, why don't you take the rope and tie it to the arm? Why do you need me?" I was sure she was toying with me.

"You are the bell ringer," she said as though it answered the question.

"Tell me, Nediam Niar, what do I do now? It is so dark I can barely see you. I'm still a good ten feet below the arm."

"Aren't you an American? Can't you rope a steer?"

Lasso it! Of course. I tied a slip knot and hit the arm on the first cast. I pulled it tight. I tugged on the rope, but the bell hardly moved in the cradle. Just that little tug pulled me off balance. To steady myself, I put all my weight on the rope. The bell pivoted somewhat in its cradle. As it pivoted back, I couldn't maintain my position on the beam and so I swung across the tower holding onto the rope. From there I had no choice. Hand over hand I lowered myself down the rope. At the floor I let go. Relieved of my weight, the bell swung back, and the clapper hit. The gong jarred my teeth.

The sun burst out. It was Easter morning.

The whole village buzzed with the story of the mountain climber that climbed the steeple. I tried to explain the part Nediam played, but for some reason they couldn't place her. She had to be a villager, I explained. I asked Four and the doctor to help me locate her. They simply smiled and busied themselves organizing the celebration, the village feast. I spent my day equally helping with the preparations and searching for Nediam.

Monday morning first thing, the twins showed up on the doorstep to tell me the car had somehow fixed itself; there would be no charge, and I was free to continue my travels. Four explained that she would be hounded from the village if she took payment from the bell ringer. In fact, she had fixed a lunch I could take with me. Try as I might to explain that she had done more than I could expect in saving me from the storm, I could not get her to take a cent.

Four, the doctor and the twins walked me up the hill to my car. I was disappointed that Nediam Niar wasn't there. I noticed a note scrawled on the windshield. "Nediam Nair, evol. nni eht ta kcab era uoY." It was backwards, but I could recognize the words "You are back at the inn." It was signed, "Love, Rain Maiden." The old woman at the bridge? No wonder the sheen live forever.

The dining room was full of my fellow climbers discussing the wonderful weather for ascending the Cuillins on this Easter week.

CHAPTER TWO

As in much of the ancient world, waves of tribal conquerors have swept across the Hebrides. We have the ancient Iberians, various tribes of the Celts including an invasion of the Irish Celts, and various groups of Viking raiders that actually established settlements and intermarried with the Celts. The fantasy characters of island lore are similar to; but not quite the same, as those that exist in the folklore of these conquerors. From the Norse we get the Trows (Trolls) and Fisher Folk, from the Celts the Water Horse or Water Kelpie and the little folk of the hills, the Sheen, that we met previously in the Rain Maiden. The Water Kelpie is often pictured in Celtic art. The animal is a shape changer, and in its water-world embodiment is shown as a scaly beast not unlike the Loch Ness Monster. It is considered by many as the likely origin of that much-sighted creature.

This water horse, most often pictured in his horse or lake monster shapes, was also known as a universal shape changer who could impersonate a human if needs be. This lycanthropic behavior made him the universal villain.

Again we return to the Isle of Skye, and find ourselves in the heart of the Cuillins, the mountains that seem to reach for the clouds. Standing alone on the shore of Loch Coruisk, a freshwater lake that literally dumps into the sea, I could easily imagine a water horse watching me. Could this devilish creature fit into a Scotland Yard tale? He wouldn't be so scary then.

Broadford had many B & B's, but the one I chose came with a story teller. My host didn't look the part of a chief inspector, so I will ask you to take the story he told "with a grain of salt," so to speak.

Baptism with a Meal

During the Second World War the population learned to eat horse meat

There seems to be no end of troublesome creatures that inhabit the Celtic world. There are the well-known ones, the mermaids and the leprechauns. Then there are the lesser known selkies, fir darrig (rat boy), and beans-idhe, better known as the banshee. We laugh at these imaginary creatures and tell scary stories fashioned on their supposed exploits. No one laughs at the water kelpie! Commissioned by Satan himself, this water horse can be found pictured on Celtic artifacts, shown in ancient writings and enshrined as the Loch Ness Monster. This beast is empowered by Lucifer to drown his victim, then eat the body and send the soul directly to hell.

We had one posing as a saint.

The Isle of Skye was named after the Norse word for 'cloud' for its high peaks seem to stretch from the ocean to the heavens. The Isle is cut in two by the Black and Red Cuillins, shale mountains that have been drawing mountain climbers and tourists to the island for hundreds of years.

Our story started when a pair of young American mountain climbers, Alex Brown and Andy Moore, returned in panic via the eight mile trek through Glen Sligachan to the inn at Sligachan and called the police. They then told the constable a crazy story of meeting St. Columba and losing the third member of their party, Matt Goodwin, during a baptism. When I received the call in Aberdeen, I thought it was a joke, but the Constable swore that as crazy as it sounded, it was their story.

I told him to have them stay at the inn, and I would be there to question them in the morning. He replied that one could stay at the inn, but the other was obviously in shock and had been taken to the clinic in Broadford and would likely overnight there.

Since the incident involved the death of one of the participants, I started for the inn immediately. It had been a long day so I thanked my lucky stars for the good road and dry weather all the way to Kyle of Lochalsh. I spent the night at the fine hotel there and crossed over to Skye on the early car ferry first thing in the morning.

Alex Brown was the climber that stayed at the inn to await my arrival. His story was incredible, to say the least. It seems that the three of them, Alex, Andy, and Matt had started out from the inn three days before. They hiked all day to arrive early in the evening at a fresh water loch, Loch Coruisk, that dumped into the ocean. There they made camp. The next morning, as they were preparing for a climb into the surrounding mountains, a stranger appeared. As though he had come out of the loch itself, the stranger emerged from the shore. He was sopping wet; his dark hair dangled down his back, and his feet were bare. Instead of passing the three of them by, he stopped and humbly bowed to them. He was dressed in a wet tonsure tied with a rope and had the look of a thoroughly drowned, ancient monk. Needless to say, he got their instant attention.

Before they recovered from the sight sufficiently to ask the obvious questions, he had pulled a loaf of bread from a bag hung over his shoulder. The bread by all odds should have been soaked with loch water, but somehow it had stayed dry. He offered to "break bread with them as a fellow Christian." The way he said it, with such dignity, was ludicrous considering his bizarre appearance from the depths of the lock.

Matt, the most gregarious of the three, responded that he had never thought of himself as a Christian. Now, he said this to stick a pin in the stranger's balloon, but the stranger took it as a challenge.

"Not a Christian? I am Saint Columba and have come to convert the heathen," he proclaimed.

"Do you do that by sharing your bread?" Matt said playfully. We were all trying our best not to laugh.

"No," said the supposed Saint, "by baptism."

"Oh, I wouldn't miss the chance to be baptized by Saint Columba himself," Matt replied enjoying the charade.

"Come with me," replied the saint, and they both walked into the water. The saint was a large fellow, a full foot taller than Matt, and one could see from the protruding arms and legs that he had a powerful build.

The constable broke into the story for the first time, "Up to this point, you still saw it as a silly charade? Did Matt go willingly into the loch?"

"He hesitated a bit because the water was cold. I think he meant to stop when he got in, say, knee deep. However, once he was in up to his knees, the stranger grabbed him around the waist and pulled him in the rest of the way."

"I was standing behind Andy," Alex noted, "so I didn't see the actual scuffle, but I heard Matt cry out as the Saint dragged him under the surface. Then both were gone. We waited for them to resurface, but a pink cloud came to the surface instead. It must have been blood! Matt's blood." Alex stopped to catch a breath. "Perhaps Andy can tell you more."

Then he continued, "Once we were sure Matt was gone, and it was not some kind of joke, we left the camping gear there and hurried back through the glen."

Now, I didn't know this lad, and so it could well be that the two boys had drowned the third. Whatever I did, I couldn't let this suspect out of my sight. "The next thing we need to do is to go back to your camping area and meet the saint and the sooner the better," I replied. "Can you make the trip back, Alex?" I asked.

Before I could get this return trip organized, a local call for the constable was diverted to the inn. He waved me over and had me pick up a second phone. It was the skipper of the excursion boat from Elgol, a small fishing port several miles by sea from Lock Coruisk. He was reporting an attack on one of his passengers by a nut case calling himself Saint Columba. Although they had driven the "saint" off, that passenger was in grave need of medical help and not just physical help. He claimed that the saint was actually a sea monster and had tried to eat him. The police had dispatched an ambulance to the dock, and one of the other constables from the island police station was on his way to Elgol to get the story first hand.

In Scotland you hear tales of all sorts of creatures, from wild animals to little folk, that prey on the unsuspecting. When these incidents are properly investigated, they turn out to have natural causes. That is to say, with a population as gullible as the Scots, it is easy to fool them with a bit of chicanery and to profit from the result even if it is only the means of a good laugh. However, murder is no joke. This "saint" had to be stopped.

The young mountain climber Alex, the constable, and I walked back over the long trail through the glen to the camp site. Once there, I realized there was a boat dock over the hill at the outlet of the loch. A quick call on a cell phone confirmed that this was the same dock that the tour boat from Elgol visited that morning.

I looked around. Where was Saint Columba?

While we were still on the trail, the other constable had arrived at Elgol and found the attacked passenger almost incoherent. You might chalk this up to the fact that he was English and therefore, naturally inscrutable. However, this was worse than the usual. He babbled something about Columba, green, and scaly. *Now, you need to remember that at this point you know more than I did. I had no idea that a kelpie was involved. Perhaps I should have realized that something malevolent was posing as the saint when no body surfaced from the climber's drowning. This did bother me, but, after all, linking this to a kelpie is a stretch of the imagination.* A search around the fresh water loch and up into the surrounding hills convinced us that our saint was nowhere in sight so we hiked back to the inn arriving late that evening.

Questioning the second climber, Andy, at the hospital the next morning added to the confusion. He described the powerful struggle that had taken place when the missing climber, Matt, was pulled under as evidenced by a huge churning of the water during the drowning. None of these stories seemed to make sense. What made the "saint" that powerful? The strength of a horse was the answer, but that explanation escaped me.

Three weeks went by, and we hadn't a clue as to whom or what had attacked the climbers or the tourist from Elgol. The Elgol ship no longer stopped at Loch Coruisk, and the trail from the inn at Sligachan was posted to discourage trekkers. One of our constables actually camped at the loch, but nothing came of it. In fact, it was over a month before the saint was encountered again. We had felt the whole matter was too ridiculous to release to the press so the people in Scotland had no warning. I blame myself for this lack of warning which allowed the saint to strike again in broad daylight.

This next appearance of our "saint" was on the island of Mull, another of the Western Isles and south of Skye. This incident took place at the ferry dock in the town of Craignure. As the ferry steamer loads, walk-on passengers without motor vehicles, some walking and some biking, wait at one side of the dock. It seems that our Saint Columba chose this time to entertain them by walking on water from a cockerel just offshore. The incident went something like this:

"You're Saint Columba? Come on now. Columba has been dead for 15 centuries," said a skeptical young tourist lassie.

"How can I convince you?" responded the saint.

"Let's see you walk on water," replied another of the young women.

The Columba impostor did! He walked all the way to the dock.

Then he reached for a helping hand and with amazing strength, pulled a young Swedish biker into the water. But that wasn't the worst of it. The onlookers swear that the saint changed shape. You guessed it. He changed to a scaly, green horse, carrying his prey down into the deep of the ocean water and not resurfacing.

There were too many witnesses to keep this appearance quiet. Luckily the onlookers boarded the ferry for Oban on the mainland and left the scene before the press arrived. Once in Oban they spread the story throughout the town. (The press later treated the incident as if it were a UFO sighting. They headlined, "Young Swedish tourist killed by Loch Ness Monster!")

Only the biker's companion, a fellow Swede, waited behind at Craignure to report formally.

Even after all this I did not relate the attack to a water kelpie. It took an outsider to clue me in.

I had flown to Mull on a helicopter to interrogate the biker's companion, the fellow Swede. By chance, an inspector from the Surete, France's equivalent of the Yard, arrived at the dock as a tourist on the return trip of the ferry. Seeing me interrogating the Swede, he stopped and offered to tell me what he had heard earlier from the departing passengers when he boarded the ferry in Oban an hour earlier.

This Frenchie introduced himself to me as Inspector Jean Baptiste. Once I had finished the interview of the Swede, I took Inspector Jean to lunch to hear his report. It was remarkably thorough. He finally reminded me of the Water Horse legend. I thought he was making a bad joke.

It was obvious that he understood because he spent a good deal of time telling me the history of the legend. It was so absurd that I started to laugh, but his expression warned me. He was serious. Could it be that the Surete believed in folk myths? I argued the nut case approach, but faced with the "walking on water" testimony, it was hard to refute the myth. Could it be? No, of course not!

Something was better than nothing, and nothing was what I had. I decided to humor Jean. "So, what do I do to stop this kelpie?" I asked?

"There is not much you can do," he replied.

"I could shoot him. That should slow him down!" I asserted.

"Not the least," replied Jean. "'No human has ever killed a water kelpie. I see that you're still skeptical," he exclaimed as he saw the look on my face. "How else do you explain the facts?"

I couldn't.

"I may be able to help," he offered. "I'm staying at Pennicamp. Look me up when and if you like."

The very next day the saint began offering baptism to tourists on Iona. By chance, one had read the local newspaper and recognized the connection with the previous day's events. He had the presence of mind to notify the owner of the guest house he was staying at, and the owner called the Mull constabulary.

One of the constables and I responded within hours, but the saint was gone. We questioned those present, but they dismissed it as a prank. Thank God no one was dragged into the water.

I decided to take Jean up on his offer for help. I didn't know what else to do. The constable and I drove to Pennicamp. There we found Jean. He had eaten at the dockside pub and was relaxing in a lawn chair watching the staked goat graze on the grass.

"Good afternoon, detective. I thought you would be back. Second thoughts on myths?" I could see the twinkle in his eye. "Sit down and enjoy the warm breeze."

"Now, I'm not saying that I buy into your kelpie explanation," I stated, "but I need to cover all angles."

"Just what other angles are you investigating?"

Now he had me. I had no other approaches. I sidestepped the question asking in return, "Say it is this creature, the demon friend of Lucifer. What can we do to stop him?"

"We need to meet with the kelpie to discuss his behavior," Jean directed.

"What, to tell him not to eat people?" I snapped back.

"No. To explain a kingdom divided against itself," he responded. Then, warming to the subject he continued, "Arrange an event, a Columba tour on the Iona beach by supposed tourists. Get a half dozen of the locals to join in the charade. Advertise with posters on the ferry docks at Fionnphort, Oban and Craignure. Set the date for next weekend. The poster should read, *'Come and follow the footsteps of the Great Saint. A walk with Columba on the remote beaches of Iona'*."

"But if he shows up, what do we do?" I asked incredulously.

"We could talk with him," he asserted. "We could point out the error of his behavior. Put an end to the saint routine. Let him know we are on to him. And we might even baptize him," Jean said, with the same twinkle in his eye.

Well, I thought, even if it is a hoax, we still might catch this saint bloke. Then we will see what we will see.

I rushed to get posters made and to recruit local law enforcement friends to play the tourist roles. We set the meeting place on a remote beach of the island of Iona and showed a simple map on the posters to locate it.

The week seemed to fly by. Early that weekend morning we arrived at the Iona beach. I was caught by surprise at the turnout of authentic tourists. We had over a hundred all waiting for the "walk with Columba." At first I wondered who would be so foolish as to come to a remote beach to meet a saint that had been dead for fifteen centuries, but from their accent, I discovered that they were all English. No wonder, I thought.

As if by cue, we also had our baptizing water kelpie in his saint disguise materialize by the water's edge. He simply couldn't miss the opportunity to show off. He strode boldly from the surf up the beach to meet us as if greeting a group of ardent fans. I guess that was understandable considering that is just what the tourists were, his fans.

He seemed ready to take over the tour director's position when Jean stepped in. "Ah, Collum Cille," he said addressing him by the saint's Gaelic name. "Baptizing away the people's sins? You were a Bible scholar in Ireland if I remember correctly," Jean said loudly for all to hear. The kelpie modestly agreed, not wanting to lose his standing in the eyes of the crowd. "And you baptize in the name of God," I believe.

Again the kelpie agreed, "I do!"

"Are you familiar with the saying in the Book of Mark? But, of course you are. Let me tell it to our guests. Jesus said, 'In truth I tell you, all human sins will be forgiven, and all the blasphemes against the Holy Spirit will never be forgiven.'"

"This," he said with a grand wave of his hand, "is Lucifer's agent baptizing in the name of God!"

Approaching the now shaken kelpie, Jean seemed to grow larger, much larger. "You are a water horse and, as such, commissioned by Lucifer himself. Each time you, the most evil of creatures, use a Christian ritual, God shakes the very pillars of hell! Good and evil must be separate; evil cannot come from good!"

"Who made you boss?" was all the kelpie could sheepishly respond.

"Lucifer!" Jean replied himself changing before our eyes into a horrific, green, scaly sea horse.

I looked to the saint, expecting him to change to his sea horse shape, but all he did was cringe as Jean or Jean the kelpie snatched him up and dove into the surf. There was an immense churning with a huge waterspout shooting into the air and showering down on the on-looking crowd. Then as quickly as it had started, the eruption stopped and for a moment all was deathly quiet. Both of the devil's creatures were gone.

I was astonished when the English tourists responded. "Jolly good show," they cheered in unison.

CHAPTER THREE

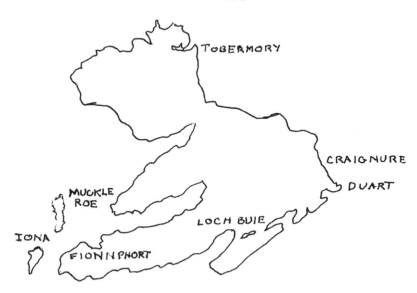

The islands we have talked about so far are the easiest to reach. They are part of a grouping called the Inner Hebrides. Yet, at the time, they were still remote. Traveling on Mull all those years ago, I was approaching Tobermory, the largest village. My mission was to find the Dwarfie Stone that overlooks the port.

I stopped at a roadside turnaround and walked across the roadway to where a young man was sitting on a log. Today, I would have called him a boy since he was in his mid-twenties, but fifty years ago, he was a man to me. I started to ask him if he knew where the Dwarfie Stone was and then noticed that he was blind. What a foolish thing to do. Could a blind man see the stone? A feeling of guilt left me speechless.

I had been driving all morning and actually needed a break. With his permission, I sat down beside him. After a moment of silence, we eased into conversation about his island. He was knowledgeable and had obviously traveled the large island from end to end. He spoke of the views as if he had seen them himself. I asked him if he was totally blind. He noted that he saw colors and shapes. He asked me to repeat the question about the *stane*, as he called it.

Calling a large standing stone by the name of a creature is a Scottish pastime. There are endless stories of members of the fairy kingdom turned to stone by Druids or sorcerers. Since there are thousands of standing stones, there is no end of named stones, and 'Dwarfie' is one of the more popular appellations.

I had the guide book, and so, with the actual detail of that Dwarfie stone, I could tell him what I was looking for. He not only described the location of the stone but also gave me directions to find it. "How can you describe the area if you are blind?" I asked.

He told me the blindness was a recent occurrence.

I asked him if it was caused by an accident. It was a dumb question because he had no other facial disfigurement. He let me off the hook by saying it was a disease that had blinded him for life. I pressed on, and he told me that two years ago a dentist had been making his yearly visit to the island to fix the teeth of all comers and had stopped the dental work long enough to examine his eyes. The verdict was cataracts which, even then, could have been easily corrected if an eye surgeon could be found. I told him this, and he said the closest one was in Glasgow, too far for him to travel. So much for the beauty of isolation.

In those days the people on Mull were still sending their children off island to the mainland to foster parents that housed them for the school year so they could go to school there.

There are several smaller islands close to Mull, but the one I found most interesting is the Isle of Iona. Revered by the Druids, Iona was Christianized around the year 500 AD by Irish monks under the leadership of Columba and became his island headquarters as he and his fellow monks carried the Gospel to the heathen Picts. It is an island that exudes peace. A magical place, it is the burial place of the kings of four countries. Yet, for us Mac-Leans, Iona is part of our heritage, one of our island home lands.

Today, the sky is bright, and the weather mild with an air so fresh that it tastes good. Sitting on a bench in front of the small Iona cathedral I can relax and reflect back to my very first visit to my ancestral homelands. Let's see now, "Why did I come here?"

Muckle Roe

From the time when as children we asked our mothers to look under the bed, fear of the unknown has been met with a lack of desire to investigate. Leave well enough alone

In the uprising of the '45, or actually in 1746, Scottish hopes were buried in holes dug in the turf of the grazing land at Culloden. The bodies of the bravest and best of Scots' manhood were separated into piles by tartan and thrown into the pits. Large stones were rolled over the filled graves to prevent family members from claiming the bodies of their kin for decent burial.

Not all Scots fought on the Jacobite side. Some, such as the MacLeods, took no side while others, such as Argyll and the Campbells, fought with Gloucester and the English. Although the subjugation of the clans had begun long before the '45, the Jacobite clans were now disenfranchised, their lands seized, and for the most part, they were forced to flee. Much of the land fell into the hands of absentee landlords who employed pseudo lawmen to force the tacksmen, crofters, and peasants from the property. Once the land was "cleared," it was turned to hunting acreage or sheep grazing to supply wool for the English mills.

Many of the smaller of the Western Isles were left vacant including, in some cases, the emptying of whole villages that had served as local commerce centers. One such fishing village on Muckle Roe had finally been vacated en mass in the year 1802, having slowly lost its market over a five decade span. It was from this very village that my family fled, first to Skye and from there across the Atlantic to Prince Edward Island, off the coast of Canada.

I was in my mid-twenties nearly fifty years ago when I decided to travel to the abandoned island and explore the village. That visit had such an impact on me that I can remember it in detail, minute by minute, as though it were yesterday.

I flew to Prestwick Airport, biked to Glasgow and took the Western Highlands Railway to Oban where I stayed the night in a bed and breakfast. The city is a seaport, and I spent the evening on the docks admiring the trawlers and breathing in the fishy salt air.

The next morning I boarded the Caledonian MacBrayne ferry and steamed northwest to the island of Mull. I biked from the dock at Craignure to Pennicamp, a bed and breakfast that sat on a nearby hill. Unfortunately, the weather had changed, and a drizzle made the walk to the local pub for dinner a miserable trek.

The next day I visited the Muckle Roe caretaker in Tobermory, the largest village on Mull, and received permission to tour the island. He was a great help in providing information on the layout of the island. It seems that it was actually the tip of a misplaced foothill of an ancient mountain chain. As it appeared above the waterline, it was simply a wedge-shaped hill sticking out of the ocean. It was some four miles long and a mile wide. For those that want to look it up on a map, it is located off the west of Mull, not far from Fionnphort. On Muckle Roe's far side, there was a natural harbor. This protected anchorage had once made it the fishing center for the area, thus giving it importance far greater than earned by its land mass. The island's proximity to Iona, Scotland's prominent sacred island, caused the village to raise a church disproportionate in size to the community rather than be outdone by its neighbor. The keeper noted that the church was still standing and infrequently used for special services requiring a smaller edifice than the present cathedral on Iona.

Unfortunately, over the years since 1800 the sea had risen some eight feet inundating part of the village and submerging the many harbor docks, creating a treacherous landing for boats attempting to unload on the village shore. To avoid this trap, people visiting the island must land on the near side. This can be done by taking the Fionnphort to Iona LST and asking the captain to make an unscheduled stop on that Muckle Roe shore. From there, a person would be required to walk the four miles up and over the hill to get to the village of the same name at the other end of the island. Actually, very few people visited the island for it had no special scenery, and the village was an abandoned ruin.

My plan was simple. Have the early ferry drop me at the near shore to spend the day on Muckle Roe and then meet the last ferry in the evening to continue on to the island of Iona where I had made arrangements to stay and spend the rest of the week exploring.

As planned, the very next day I bussed from the ferry dock at Craignure to Fionnphort and left on the first ferry for Iona. In my pack I had lunch, water, and rain gear. The ferryman dropped me on the near side of Muckle Roe. It was agreed that I would meet the last ferry run of the day at the same point that evening to complete the trip to Iona.

The day was overcast, which heightened the feeling of adventure. As we approached, the island seemed dark and mysterious. On the hillside I could see the remains of a graveyard. In contrast to the uplifting of spirits that seem to occur effortlessly when one reaches Iona, the feelings of loneliness and, I must admit, foreboding seemed to permeate the island of Muckle Roe. Had it always been this way? No wonder it was abandoned.

Actually it wasn't abandoned. There were sheep everywhere.

Walking the length of the island was a long, uphill climb for the land peaked near the village end. I set my mind to the task at hand and began picking my way across the craggy landscape. The slope provided drainage, so the hike avoided the boggy landscape that covered much of the flatter islands. On the dry ground, I made good time and arrived at the crest mid-morning. Below I could see the main street of the village. It ran parallel to the shore. There had been houses and perhaps shops on both sides of the street, but the rising water and stormy seas had claimed the seaward portion of the buildings and left little on that side, other than the church, which appeared intact. On the inland side of the roadway, the buildings still stood tall, some twenty by quick count. Although the thatch was long gone, much of the wood and all of the stone still remained. For the most part, the wooden structural pieces had been fashioned from drift wood which had already withstood the ravages of the sea and now still stood against the storms. Doors, whose hinges had long ago rusted through, lay in position, and driftwood rafters indicated the missing roof lines.

However, the striking feature wasn't the remaining houses but, rather, the church. As I had been told, it was intact even though its foundation now extended into the sea. It was a large structure of a surprising character. It looked like a miniature castle with parapets and all. Yet, inside this facade was the sloping roof of the church proper towering above the walls. From the ground and from the town it would resemble a castle. The only view of the actual sloped roof was from this hill. This roof was slate and looked to be in good condition. It was obvious that the building was maintained. At the far point of the roof was a white figure, I guessed of Christ. This statue stood looking down on twelve smaller figures. These were actually drains for the roof to channel rain water from the parapets far out from the walls to fall directly to the earth below without creating erosion of the walls. I guessed those figures to be the twelve disciples kneeling in prayer.

For some unknown reason, the church made me feel uneasy, so I delayed my examination of it until mid-afternoon, preferring to spend my time in the village. The houses still contained much of the handmade furniture although it was rotted beyond repair. The iron cookware coated with carbon and grease had fared much better and was reclaimable. There was a good deal of rigging lying about along with tools of all kinds. Yet, there was nothing which differentiated one dwelling from another with the exception of the few shops and an iron monger's workroom. Nothing was left that identified the actual owners of the individual buildings. There was no evidence directly related to my family.

Mid-afternoon, having exhausted my curiosity regarding the village, and realizing that my time was running out, I finally turned to the church. From below it was hard to see the figures on the parapets so I began my inspection by climbing the front steps. I was disappointed to see that there was no sign to announce the name or original denomination. The doors were huge, some twenty feet high and a full ten feet across. The latch was a large ring that turned and drew a bolt so the door could swing outward. The ring turned freely, and the bolt slid back. The door was less obliging. It took all my strength to open it a foot or so, just enough to allow me to squeeze in. Then, with an unnerving thud, it slammed shut behind me.

The first thing I felt was the cold. I pulled out a wool sweater from my pack. To my surprise, there were no pews. The windows were small and plain with empty candle holders below the sashes. There were no statues in the church, no burial vaults, and no inscriptions on the floor or walls. There was an altar but no cross, no candles, and no font. Although it was a bit dark inside, there was sufficient light to assess the condition of the nave. It appeared to be in good repair and clean. The exception was the altar. Dark brown stains soaked the stone slab, extending in rivulets down the sides. The nave was not huge, but the lack of pew furniture made it seem larger. As I had said, the church was disproportionate to the size of the village.

Each step I took echoed off the bare stone walls. Every few steps I would stop to see if there were other steps echoing beside mine, and, thankfully, there were not. I could not shake an evil feeling that I was being watched. I braved it out and continued on.

The lack of decoration made the rest of my tour of the church proper relatively short. I noticed that there was a partially opened door to one side of the altar. There was a cold draft coming from it. Curiosity pushed me on to step into the passageway. This led to what had probably been a vesting room, a sacristy, but the wardrobes were gone, and the room was as bare as the church. The one exception was a round iron ring in the center of the floor with a set of leg and neck manacles attached. Had this room been a cell? Who would have been held prisoner in a church? The room was unusually musty and chillingly cold.

There was another door ajar in the far corner of the room. This opened on a staircase. As I stepped across the threshold, I realized that this was the source of the inordinate cold. Yet, I couldn't see any cause for the chilling draft.

I reasoned that the chill must have been in my mind for the stairs plainly led up to the parapets and outdoors. Even on this dark, sunless day, the fresh outside air would still be warm from the summer's heat.

There was no question that heights bothered me. I suffered from height sickness. Yet, it was the conquering of this fear that made mountain climbing one of my hobbies. This fear caused me to pause, and again the oppressive nature of the place overwhelmed me.

I think it must have been the debate my mind went through regarding the height sickness fear that distracted me sufficiently to keep the dread from turning me back. After what seemed like minutes, I was able to override the fear and force myself up the staircase. The door at the top opened on to the parapets. I clenched my teeth and stepped out. You can only begin to imagine the shock when I found myself face to face with a hideous, forked-tail devil, carefully carved from a block of stone some three feet long. It stood out from the wall face, with a hollow body and a mouth with tongue extended to project the roof runoff far out from the outer wall. A quick glance told me that all twelve of the statues I has seen from the hill were gargoyles, similar devils to the first with the exception of the forked tail. That was reserved for the first gargoyle only, some mark of rank perhaps. These ancient figures were as perfect in detail as the day they were carved. There were no signs of the wear and tear I would have expected from one hundred and fifty years of neglect.

I turned to the "Christ" figure I had seen at the peak of the roof only to realize that it could not be Jesus. It seemed to have wings. It was so eroded that it was hard to be sure, but probably had portrayed an angel keeping watch over the devilish brood below. The reason for the difference in appearance and erosion could be explained by the premise that the keeper didn't want to walk on the slate portion of the roof to reach the angel for restoration work.

Had the builders of this church been trying to scare the villagers into belief, to show them a vision of hell? I remembered the gargoyles on the church in Stirling. But where were the corresponding figures for heaven? Not up here, and not in the bare church below. These hellish figures were not all the same, but they were all hideous. Especially my fork-tailed friend, but as I looked again I realized that it wasn't forked. Ahead of me I saw that it was the third gargoyle that had the forked tail. How had I become confused? Had they changed places? Of course not! Yet, I felt that something was just about to happen.

I moved on along the walkway from gargoyle to gargoyle wondering at the fine features and excellent condition of these horrors. Looking to the west through the overcast, I realized that the evening was approaching. At this time of year the days were long. Yet, I needed to make my way back across the island and be waiting when the last ferry arrived. I couldn't waste time here. As I hurried back across the parapet to the door way, I had a strong premonition that movement was taking place. To my dismay I noted statue one by the doorway was now my fork-tailed figure again. Without looking back, I entered the landing, pulled the door shut and descended the stone staircase. The fear seemed to follow me, and my mind conjured a view of the creatures in pursuit.

What was this? I lost my composure completely upon entering the robing room. The manacles were no longer empty. A live goat was wearing them. Who had put the goat there while I was above?

I raced through the robing room into the church slamming the sacristy door behind me. Light from window candles caused me to stop in my tracks. The holders had been empty, but now each contained a burning candle. "Hello," I cried, without receiving an answer. Was this an evening when the congregation from Iona was using the church? Were a few of the acolytes at work as an advanced party to get the place ready? Why didn't they answer when I called? No, this was something far more sinister than an evening Eucharist.

There was a commotion behind the closed door to the robing room.

I charged up the aisle of the nave to the large wooden doors. The bar was still disengaged. All I had to do was push, and I did. The door would not budge. Now there were footsteps coming up the aisle behind me. With all the echoes it sounded like a throng. There was no time to look back. I put my shoulder to the door, and slowly it moved outward. It seemed to be inching out. Were those hands grabbing at my clothes? They were pulling me back. Was I to join the goat as a sacrifice for these demons?

Finally, the opening was large enough so I could slip through. With an effort born of the adrenaline rush from the fear of capture, I pulled free, squirmed through the opening and fell backwards down the front steps. As I rolled in the dirt, the giant door slammed shut with a loud thud behind me. I was sure that at any moment it would open again and a horde of horrors pounce on me to drag me back to the ghoulish festivity.

Driven by terror, I sprang to my feet and scrambled up the hill, realizing that the further I got from the church, the safer I would be. Safe from what? Safe from the demons, from the animal sacrifice, and perhaps my own sacrifice? Were they chasing me?

Finally, out of breath, I dropped to a large rock outcrop beside the trail and looked back. As I looked far down at the church below, I wasn't surprised to find the parapets empty.

CHAPTER FOUR

From our bench seat on Iona we can look back at the island of Mull. Since we are considering the James MacLean family and its roots in the Inner Hebrides, this would be a good time to explore the tale of their curse.

There were stories that came from the old days in Scotland. My great-grandfather Samuel MacLean was a sea captain. Three of the large barques he captained sank while sailing between Scotland and Canada, and yet, somehow, he escaped from each disaster. There is no end of Sam MacLean stories including one of a voyage on which his wife and son were passengers. His young son was still nursing on goat's milk. The ship was sinking, and Sam, his young family, and the crew were safe aboard life boats rowing for shore when Sam's wife, Kate, insisted that he go back onto the sinking ship to get the goat.

It would be Sam's generation that would tell the following tale. They were the guardians of the old stories. So find a comfortable seat, and let my great-grandfather begin.

The Dark Horseman

Heads, you lose

Buddy thump, buddy thump, buddy thump, buddy thump, and buddy thump.

"Sam, do ye hear that? It's the dark horseman! You have not to fear. He's not here for you. You are far too young. Perhaps he has come for me." My favorite grandfather looked tired.

Now I need to explain the significance of the dark horseman to you, my friend.

The Maclaines of Lochbuie are a branch of the MacLeans of Duart. All Mac-Leans, no matter how you spell it, consider themselves descendants of Gillean of the Battle Axe, a fierce warrior of the Thirteenth Century who fought in the battle of Largs in 1263. Black John, Gillian's great-grandson, had two sons, Hector and Lachlan. At John's death, Lachlan was granted the lands of Duart, including the family castle of that name, and Hector the lands of Lochbuie, where he built a castle. Thus they shared the MacLean lands on the Isle of Mull between them and each became a chief of a clan branch. Just five generations later the then chief, Iain Og, the fifth Laird of Lochbuie, had a son that envied his father's wealth. That son, Ewan, went to mounted battle against his father who, in the course of the struggle, beheaded him. From that day forward all members of the Lochbuie branch of the clan are on guard against the headless one, Ewan, who, if allowed, will take their lives.

"I'll chase him away, Seanar," I said to my grandfather with my childish bravado.

"Noo, Noo, you'll not do that."

"Why?" I was hurt. I was nearly a man. Why couldn't I be trusted to drive him away?

Seanar saw my hurt. "It isn't my time," he said. "You don't see him here, do you? Bad things can come from challenging the headless one. When I was your age, my mother was ill from the fever. That is what we called influenza. My father considered it his job to keep the dark horseman away from our home. But now he had to ride to Tobermory, fifteen miles, for the doctor. Would the horseman come while he was gone?

He started before day break just as soon as he could see the road. He didn't say, 'You stand guard Murdock.' He made no charge at all. It was clear that he still saw me as a child, which perhaps I was.

My mother was very feeble. I spent much of the day waiting on her as I had for more than a week. She was a courageous woman and not one to complain, but she had developed a fever and could not wait on herself. She was only semi-conscious that day.

As the day wore on, I could see the change in her. The fever increased, and by mid-afternoon she would no longer swallow the cool water I brought her. If only the doctor were here, I thought. What if the dark rider should come?

My mother was the first one to hear him.

Buddy thump, buddy thump, buddy thump, buddy thump, buddy thump.

He was far off down the pass on the old road. 'Allen, he is coming!' she cried to my father, not knowing he was gone.

What should I do, I thought?

Then I saw the rifle over the mantle. Just last month my father had shown me how to use it. It was far too big for me, but his father had shown him at a young age so he felt he should do the same. I don't think he expected me to use it for many years, but he took the time, and it made me feel like a man. Perhaps he understood my desire to be a man rather than the child I was.

I took it down, went to the drawer, and filled the clip with shells. I inserted the loaded clip into the rifle. Then I went out the door and waited.

Buddy thump, buddy thump, buddy thump, buddy thump, buddy thump. In the evening dusk I saw him coming up the road.

I did what my father had taught me. I cocked the gun. I raised the gun to my shoulder. I pressed it hard against my shoulder muscle. Otherwise, the kick would knock me down, and I would lose the chance for a second shot if the first didn't do the job. Yes, I had time to make this a marksman's shot as I waited for the rider to come closer. I would do it step by step. I sited through the v notch. Closing my left eye, I aligned the stub at the barrel's end with the target. I took a deep breath and held it. The gun was heavy, but I centered the dot on the rider and slowly squeezed the trigger. I would hit him in the chest I thought. That should stop him.

I squeezed harder on the trigger, and it moved in the trigger guard. I tensed for the bang and squeezed with all my might. *Click*. The hammer dropped on an empty space. I had failed to chamber a shell from the clip into the breech.

I had time for a second try but stopped in horror. Dear God, it was my father returning! I had almost shot my father! All I could do was cry when he arrived. I could not tell him my error. He took the crying to the fact that the doctor had not come back with him.

'The fever is in the village, too. The good doctor is coming as soon as he can.'

That evening we heard hoof beats. 'Thank God; the doctor has arrived,' my father said as he opened the door wide. There stood the headless horror! My mother, your great-grandmother, was dead."

My grandfather sat there, head bowed, for several minutes caught in the mood of his own story. Then he looked up at me and said, "Noo, today is not my day."

Buddy thump, buddy thump, buddy thump, buddy thump, buddy thump.

CHAPTER FIVE

If Imagination is the child, then Curiosity is the mother. One could spend a lifetime in the islands of the Inner Hebrides without exhausting the discoveries. However, the Minch, the inner waterway between the Outer and the Inner Hebrides, is a porous barrier, and sooner or later, the attractions of the Outer Hebrides were bound to drag me across. I was particularly drawn by the most compelling site of all the island artifacts, the Stones of Callanish. There is no end of theories explaining this large collection of stones located at the Head of Loch Roag on the Isle of Leodhas, (pronounced Lewis). From a distance the collection looks like a hill top covered with stubs of telephone poles. In fact, once there, one sees not just one collection but others on promontories for miles around. Early studies of the principal stone formation found an alignment with true north within one degree. Remember that four thousand years ago there was no pole star to use as a guide. That alignment was an unbelievable feat.

So I traveled by train to Mallaig and from there by ferry to Lochboisdale on South Uist. Then I traveled north through the islands of Benbecula and North Uist. These islands were low and wet, dotted with small lochs and covered with peat. Here and there were ancient ruins. Perhaps the most common were the cairns, piles of loose stones, which stood out on many hilltops. These cairns had various uses, but the ones of interest to us are the hollow, chambered ones. Exploration of several of those cavernous rock piles led to the following ramble.

The Body in the Bag

Watch carefully, and see if you can pick the shell that hides the bean. Now this is a shell game, and you need to listen carefully because at the story's end you will be asked to identify **the body in the bag**

Willie MacLeod was a true Scot. When he wasn't crewing on a trawler, he was outside his cottage playing the pipes. As a true Scot, he saved every cent he made and died a wealthy man. He had no family, and all close kin had died before him. So, all that hard-earned money would go to the Crown. That is, all except the money needed to bury him.

Willie's testament required a very special burial routine, common practice in the days of old. In past centuries, in the Outer Hebrides, death was the start of a journey that could take days to complete.

In those early times, after proper preparation, the corpse would be transported either by hand or cart to the nearest burial cairn in the direction of travel. There it would stay until transporters from the next town or island in the chain claimed it and moved the body to the next cairn. Then, again there it would stay until claimed by the next transporters and so forth until it arrived for final interment at the family or clan burial ground on the specific island that the family considered the ancestral home.

Willie's will specified a modified version of the historical routine. His corpse was to be handled in the old way, carried from the mortuary to a cairn by horse cart. The body, in a body bag, would be placed in the cairn's chamber overnight while the horse and drivers overnighted at a nearby inn. From there it would slowly proceed, not to the next cairn, nor to the family grave site, but to the *Molly Rose* for burial at sea. From Balivanich on Benbecula to Lochmaddy on North Uist, routes 892 to 865 and on to 867, a two hour drive by auto at most, would become a two day procession by horse-drawn cart.

Everett Broadbent was master of ceremonies, the virtuoso of the mortuary, the Mozart of the dirge, and above all, the only undertaker on Benbecula. Well-prepared, the body would be consigned to the care of two brothers, the Toms, Tom the older and Tom the younger, twins born minutes apart. Unlike the past shuttle runs, when a body was taken to the cairn for the night to be picked up and carried by the inhabitants of the next town, the Toms were to transport the body the full distance.

The Toms were selected for good reason. Simple-minded, they had not been able to qualify for drivers' licenses so they traveled by cart pulled by an old mare they called 'Horse.' The two Toms were slow-witted. So slow, in fact, that people who knew them said, "If brains were dynamite, neither of the Tom's would have enough to blow his nose." In tune with their abilities, the instructions were simple. *"Take the body, which would be placed in a black bag, to the cairn at Barpa Langass, and then spend the night at the Langass Inn, about a mile from the cairn. Finally, the next morning, take the body from the cairn to the pier at Lochmaddy. There the crew of the 'Molly Rose' would take it for its final trip to the sea burial."*

Unfortunately, Willie wasn't Broadbent's only customer that weekend. Big John MacKinnon, the island's kingpin of crime, had died suddenly of a heart attack. Should word get out that he was dead, all the petty crooks in the outer isles would be deserting the ship. Big John was hated, feared and adored by the evil element of the isles. It was his meanness that kept out the really bad crooks from the mainland.

Big John's organization operated on the basis of terror. It was well-known that MacKinnon was a mean bugger that enjoyed a perfect record. All who had dared to oppose him lost their health and sometimes their lives. In addition, if Big John's "customers" should hear of his death, it would set them free. His second in command, Little John, realized that he must not let his neighbors know Big John was dead.

Little John needed to get rid of the body. Pitch it into the sea on the outgoing tide, it would be months before it would wash up on the mainland, and no one would recognize the decomposed body, he rationalized. The McGee's, small time hoodlums, have a pickup truck. They could do the dirty work.

In Benbecula, Broadbent had a small embalming shop. Prepared and bagged bodies were usually placed in coffins. Then they were moved to a loading dock behind the shop. Both Willie's body and Big John's were to be bagged but not coffined. In Willie's case, it was to cut down on size and weight for handling purposes. The cairns would not hold coffin size packages. Big John was destined to be thrown into the sea. A coffin would attract attention and possibly float. So both would be bagged, but neither would be coffined.

As the first body was completed, the package was placed on the dock. This was just moments before the Toms arrived. They loaded it on their cart. "A bit heavier than he looked," Tom the older remarked.

An hour later the second body was completed and placed on the dock. The two McGee brothers loaded it into their pickup. Now it wasn't a prize job assignment so Little John MacKinnon had assigned two lightweights, Fletcher and Tweede MacGee. The two drove the pickup a few miles north to the causeway across Eilean Bay and threw the body in. From there they reasoned, it should wash out on the tide.

Reporting back to Little John they noted that the tide was high, and, as expected, the lowering of the tide would carry the body to a grave far out in the sea.

"Did anyone see you?" Little John asked.

"No, sir. We parked on the right side of the causeway and pulled the body out along the right-hand side of the truck. The pickup shielded us," they explained with a bit of pride. "Then we slid the bag into the water just as nice as you please."

"On the right side of the road!" exclaimed Little John. "That's the inside, the Minch side of the island. As the tide goes out, he'll end up back on shore beside the causeway!"

Little John was beside himself with anger. "Go back and move him to the other side. Then the tide can carry him out to sea!" he sputtered. What had made him choose these two clowns, he thought? They couldn't even find the sea.

Within fifteen minutes, the McGee brothers were back at the causeway just in time to cross paths with the Toms. "Look, they have the body! Now what do we do? They must have found it and are taking it in their cart to the police on Uist," Tweede cried.

"We'll have to follow them and steal it back," said Fletcher.

Now, we need to stop the story here to explain that as dumb as this might seem, there is something to be said for this solution. You see, we don't know whose body is on the cart. It could be Big John's. Remember it was a bit heavy. Stealing it back could at least solve one problem.

"Yes, sir, what can we do for you?" asked Tom, the older, as a man approached from a pickup pulled to the side of the road.

Tweede McGee explained that his pickup wouldn't go. "Someone must have stolen the engine."

"Really, you're not kidding?" asked Tom the younger.

"No, sir, come; see." While the two brothers walked to the front of the pickup, Fletcher slid the body off their cart and loaded it in the back of the truck.

Tweede lifted the hood. Tom the older pointed and said, "There it is."

"That's the engine?" replied Tweede.

"Sure is."

"Well, thanks for finding it for us," said Tweede.

"Don't mention it." said Tom the older.

The two Toms walked back to their cart and gave Horse the signal to "get along." They drove the cart past the pickup never thinking to look at what it was hauling.

"What now?" asked Fletcher. "We can't dump the body with those two in sight. It will take them all afternoon to get across the causeway."

"We'll drive on and dump it on the Atlantic side of Uist," Tweedy concluded. And that was just as well for the Toms were about to turn back.

It wasn't more than a mile later that Tom the younger remarked, "Tom, the body must have fell out."

"What makes you say that?" asked the older.

"It's gone."

So the Toms started to retrace their steps back across the causeway. "Look, it's over there. It must have rolled into the water. Stop, and I'll pull it out and load it back on," said Tom the younger. He was the strong back of the weak-brained duo.

Here again it appears that fortune may have smiled for both transporters have bodies onboard that seem to be the ones they should have started with. Well, as they say, don't start counting your chickens.

Both transporter teams had bodies. It was dusk. The two crooks, the Mc-Gees, had driven to North Uist and were parked by the edge of the road discussing the best place to relaunch their body. Now the story ought to end here, but Norbert, the friendly patrol man, motor cycle and all, pulled up beside the truck to join the talk. He had been hiding in the parking area for Barpa Langass, a large, well-preserved, chambered cairn, taking his late afternoon nap.

"Oh, no, It's Norbert," Fletcher warned. They knew he would look in the back of the pickup sooner or later.

While Fletcher kept Norbert busy, Tweede excused himself, "to take a leak" and sneaked around back to pull the body off. He dragged it down the roadside, across the road and up a long incline, stowing it in the chamber of the Barpa Langass cairn. The whole thing was done so quietly that he had not attracted Norbert's gaze. Then, he returned to the truck.

Finally, conversation over, the McGee's drove off realizing that they would have to return once Norbert was gone and pick up the body again. "We'll play it safe and wait 'til dark," Tweede remarked.

At dusk the two Toms arrived at the Cairn and shoved their bundle into the chamber. In the dark they didn't see the other occupant.

Langass Inn, not a mile away, had finnan haddie that night, and the Toms didn't want to miss it. You could smell it cooking a mile away, an aroma sweet to the hearts of all Scots, best described as the sour smell of vinegar by non-Scots.

Again fate stepped in, for old Horse had pulled his last load, and so died as they entered the inn's parking lot. They unhitched the traces and dragged his body around the side of the inn. There they covered him with a tarp. They discussed it with the innkeeper who made a phone call and then assured them that the knacker man would come the next morning to claim the horse's body.

Next, Tom the older called Broadbent. "He's dead," he noted, and Broadbent immediately agreed.

"The knacker will be here in the morning to take care of the body."

Broadbent was startled. "No, take him to the *Molly Rose*."

Well, that took Tom by surprise. "What would the *Rose* do with a dead horse?" Tom asked.

"The horse? Oh, your horse is dead! Why didn't you say so?" And then, "Where is the body?"

"Horse?"

"No, Willie!"

"In Langass Cairn."

Recovering from his confusion, Broadbent noted that he would pass the cairn on his way home. He told Tom the Older that he would simply stop and collect the body, placing it in the back of his hearse. Then, in the morning, he would take it to the *Rose* himself. No one would ever know the difference. The two Toms could spend the night at the inn and return home in the morning. He was sorry to hear about the horse, but their pay would help them to buy another.

Broadbent closed his shop, and in less than a half hour, he arrived at the parking lot, walked up the hill, pulled the body from the cairn and began dragging it to the hearse. Before he got to the hearse, the two crooks in the pick-up bounced into the parking lot to retrieve their bundle of joy.

In the glow of their headlights they saw a man loading a bag into the back of a hearse. "Hey, he's got our body," said Tweede.

As the hearse drove out of the lot, Fletcher noted, "It's Broadbent. Maybe the boss has asked him for help."

It took several minutes for the obvious question to enter Tweede's limited mind. "I wonder how he knew where the body was? Let's go to the inn and call the boss. Broadbent must have been following us. He is double-crossing Little John. Planning blackmail, I bet."

The next morning a body in a bag was on the dock, waiting pickup by the *Molly Rose*. As the mate started to load the body on board, the customs inspector drove up. "That a body?" he asked.

"Sure is," responded the mate.

"Who's the lucky stiff? Strange cargo for the *Rose,* isn't it? Let me see the paperwork."

The mate gave him the order from the funeral home. The mate explained. "An old sea dog. You know him, Willie MacLeod. Wanted to be buried at sea. We'll take him out ten miles or so, tie a chain on and dump him over."

"Go to it," approved the inspector. "Wait, I'd better look inside the bag to be sure it's him"

"Been dead for three days. Might stink," warned the mate.

"Got to check any way, smell or not. Let's zip it open." And so they looked.

Now let's see if you were paying attention. Whose body did they find? All those who say Willie, raise their hands. All those for Big John, raise theirs. Well, you are both wrong; for you see, they found neither. It was the body of Everett Broadbent.

CHAPTER SIX

As I traveled north from Uist, through Harris and finally to the Isle of Leodhas or Lewis, I passed the Carloway Broch. Certainly, imagination could create stories from this tower ruin.

Continuing north I tried to visualize the Broch as it had once been. I can do this I thought and lapsed into day dreaming. But as fate would have it, I was derailed by a pretty face.

The Lady of Storms

No one knows from where it blows or where it goes

I consider traveling for the sake of "seeing things" a waste of time. I was still young and independent in the early 60's and looking for material for my storytelling. I had run Hawthorne, Irving and the likes to the ground and began to feel that I was still living in the 1800's. I was Scottish and related to a *Lord of the Isles* which, to my mind, qualified me as a Sennachie, a storyteller, so I looked to the Scottish Isles for my new material. The Isle of Lewis, the largest and most populous of the Outer Hebrides, was chock full of opportunities,

As some seek the unusual place, I look for the unusual person. Now, if I happen to find that person young and attractive, more's the pleasure. And so it happened on that marvelous June day on the outer coast of Lewis.

Traveling the shore road just north of Carloway, I noted, far down the hill on my left, a collection of buildings clinging to the tip of a tiny peninsula that protruded into the Atlantic. I pulled to the side of the road to get a better look. As you realize, the automobiles in Scotland are opposite-side steering wheel from those in the United States. You drive on the left rather than the right side of the road, and the driver sits on the right side of the car, the side closest to the center line of the roadway. So, to get a good look at something on your left, you must not only pull over but also step out to get a true panoramic view. When I did this, what I saw was a small fishing village perched precariously on the point of land about a mile downhill from this the main road. The buildings were all carefully whitewashed which gave them sharp contrast to the brown and green of the surrounding craggy-spined point of land and the deep blue of the ocean.

It was a sunny day with billowy clouds. The usual Atlantic blow sped the clouds across the landscape producing a kaleidoscope of patterns lighting each white structure in its turn. It was as if the buildings were lights in a flashing neon sign saying, "This is the place." I couldn't resist; I had to go down there.

At first, the one lane road to the village was steep, and within a half mile I guessed that I'd dropped a good three hundred feet. Then it flattened out as it approached the village. It had been a straight shot, so I coasted the last part of the hill and free-wheeled to the start of the houses. It made me think of tobogganing down a hill near my house in New England and sliding on for another half mile or so across the field at the bottom. Then I was into the narrow main street of the village.

I also admit to a second motive for the turn off the main road. I was hungry, and the village was a likely place for a pub. It was mid afternoon, and I had missed lunch. As it turned out, there was a pleasant-looking stone building at the tiny village square that was identified as the usual *Fisherman's Inn, Fine Food and Brew.*

It wasn't that it was so dark inside; it was the contrast with the bright sunlight that made me pause in the doorway. I could see a few villagers at the bar, but the lunch crowd, if there had been one, was gone. Then as my eyes refocused, I saw her at the table in the corner. Dark hair for a Scot, more Norman than Celt, she was looking at me as well. I turned my back on the bar and walked over to her table asking her quietly, "How is the food?"

"Good sandwiches, bakes her own bread."

What the hell I thought, "Can I join you?"

"Pull up a chair," she replied without hesitation, those dark eyes looking straight at mine.

The bartender acted as waiter, and I ordered a sandwich and an ale. My dark-haired beauty moved her collection: tea, a sandwich, and cheese, to her side of the table. "A Yank," she remarked. "What brings you here?"

"It could be you," I returned, but realizing how that sounded I quickly added, "if you can tell me something unusual about this village." Frankly, I was very attracted by those eyes but afraid that a crude approach might just get me a slap in the face. For all I knew, she was married to a Scottish giant who would smell my blood any moment now. Rather than the romantic approach, I opted for the storyteller searching for the unusual story approach which was at least half true. The explanation sounded a bit shallow, and I expected her to tell me to take a hike.

The barman brought my sandwich and ale, and I began to eat hoping she would not get up and move away. To my surprise she responded, "I'm a writer, and, yes, there is a story about this village. I've written it. Would you like to hear it?"

Now you have probably read her book and will remember the story. I've never seen it. Angela was her first name, but I've forgotten her last. Since this village was only a number of chapters in the book and not in the title, I have no easy way to locate the novel. If you can recollect the title, I'd appreciate having it. Then at least I could give her the proper credit. Well, to get on with it, this is the story in her own words as best I can remember.

"You couldn't imagine the ignorance of these people," she began. "In the war, the village was bombed by the Germans. It had always been a tiny place, just three hundred people. A dozen villagers, three of them young children, died that night. My mother was one of them. These people believe that the village was bombed to eliminate my mother. *The Lady of Storms* they called her." (At this point I stopped eating my sandwich and never returned to it.)

"My mother was a modern woman," she went on, "not a witch. She studied to be a mathematician and was an Assistant Professor at the University in Edinburgh. When the Second World War started, my father joined the Royal Air Corps. My mother gave up teaching and moved to the Isle of Lewis ostensibly to avoid the danger of being bombed in the air raids on the city. It wasn't until I became an adult that I was told the true reason for the move. It seems that there was a listening station on Lewis, and my mother was a code breaker.

Rather than spending her time waiting at the code center, hidden in the village mill, my mother, the only code breaker assigned to the operation, chose to work at home. The listening station monitored continuously, but intercepts were intermittent and occurred at odd hours around the clock. Only those that were intended for Berlin were translated by my mother to identify the few that should be sent to the attention of the Admiralty. The other routine messages were sent to G2 for processing.

I suppose the sight of people, non-villagers, visiting our house at odd hours fostered the story that my mother was some sort of secret agent. The villagers never did understand the purpose of the outpost at the mill.

Then, late one afternoon, the villagers spotted a suspicious ship offshore. It flew no flag of registry, and its hull was numbered rather than named. The village watch was posted around the clock since this harbor was a strategic landing point. The watch was doubled that night to continually observe the mystery ship. Late in the night they noted the lowering of a smaller boat for a landing party. The alert was spread quietly throughout the village including the mill.

The dim light used as the boat was lowered showed that the landing party was armed with rifles. This was to be a surprise attack. Warned, the listening post personnel armed and took strategic positions at the shore accompanied by a number of the Home Guard.

My mother went out without a weapon and to everyone's surprise stood on a ledge in the moonlight in clear sight of the landing party boat as it was slowly rowed towards the beach. The men in the boat stopped rowing and as if caught in slow motion, stared at her in disbelief. The other watchers remained hidden but were surely angered by her foolish act.

All of a sudden, from God knows where, a storm front swept across the bay. The fury of the wind caught the small boat broadside, swamping it. Rather than sink, the boat capsized and was driven by the gale onto the rock jetty that skirted the harbor. Men and boat were bashed, and the boat wreckage and bodies later washed up on the beach."

(I could picture her mother standing at the top of the cliff, thrusting out her hands to conjure up the huge wave that caught the small boat. It would have convinced me that she was a witch. Yet, the dark-eyed storyteller continued to deride the witnesses.)

"The villagers knew that my mother worked for the government. From the raiding party incident some of the old crones of the village concocted a myth that her service was tied to creating bad weather to keep German landing parties away from our shores.

I know that this seems hard to believe. I don't think my mother was aware of the accusations. She made matters worse by often walking on the beach in subsequent storms, seemingly fascinated by the lightning and wind. In one particular case a German patrol boat had been sighted in the adjacent harbor but was promptly driven out to sea by a ferocious blow that the wretched biddies said materialized from my mother's black magic.

Perhaps the clincher for the islanders occurred when we heard that my father's plane was shot down. The sky turned dark and storm-like and stayed that way for days; this was in June, the least stormy month of the year. The pastor called a council meeting regarding the unfortunate weather event and its supposed link to my mother's loss. As a somewhat backdoor approach to exorcism, he explained the village Free Church would hold a mock funeral. 'Put the wandering spirit to rest,' the rector advised the council, while telling my mother and me that it was a gesture of fondness by the saintly parishioners. The service was held, and the town turned out in force. As fate would have it, the sun came out directly following the recessional.

The bombing came less than a week later, and my mother was found, crushed under rubble in the village church."

(I could see the sadness in those eyes now as if this had happened that very day.)

"After her death I moved to my aunt's home in Glasgow for the remainder of the war and from there to live with my father in Tayside. He had survived the crash of his plane, escaped though Switzerland and after a few months in the hospital, had been discharged home to recuperate. The escape had ruined his health, and just two years later he died of pneumonia.

There were sufficient funds in his estate to allow me to complete my education. I followed this with the writing of two novels that were both profitable and recognized as significant writings.

Then I started the third novel. Since I published under my own name, it became easy for the public to find me and disrupt what few, truly creative moments I had. I decided to move back to this remote village my mother and I had lived in so many years before."

(She paused as if to gather her thoughts. Why would she come here of all places? I would think it was the place of bad dreams. Yet, here she was.)

She continued, "I had been named after my mother, and although grown up and much changed in appearance, the name was quickly recognized. At first I thought the villagers were just quiet or shy. When I went to church, no one would sit in the same pew with me. When I shopped, other customers cut their shopping short, leaving the store as soon as they could settle their bills. I found that my phone calls elicited curt, almost rude answers, and I had to go to the next village to get service help. I finally began to use the next village's shops, rather than the ones in my village to avoid the embarrassment. When they looked at me, did they see me or my mother?

I tried to assure people that I was not my mother reincarnated. It is hard to tell whether they accepted that or not. I felt like a leper. I met with the present pastor of the village Free Church, but he was new to the town and could not explain the strange behavior of his parishioners. He asked me to speak to the congregation the next Sunday at the tea. The large turn out surprised the pastor, for it was more common for only a few to stay after the service for refreshments.

It took all my courage to get up and speak. I told the crowd what I had learned from the Ministry regarding the fateful bombing. I reminded them that there was a listening post in the old grist mill and explained that the bombing was an attempt to destroy the post, not my mother. I insisted that my mother did not bring on the bombing and was not responsible in any way for the villagers' deaths.

They were not the only ones suffering from the raid. I explained that the events were so traumatizing for me that I suffered a loss of memory and to this day cannot remember the attack. At that there was a loud murmur as the people conferred with one another."

"All this time and you could not recall the bombing?" someone remarked.

"Yes, I could not," I answered.

"And how do you feel about this village?" another asked.

"I think it could be a very nice village," I responded.

"Could be?" another repeated.

"Yes, if you would just talk with me," I continued.

"From that time forward the village seemed to split in half. Those that accepted the truth of my message and those that did not. At least now half the village spoke to me."

(Then there was a long, reflective pause as if she were weighing alternatives. Suddenly the eyes were no longer sad. The pleasant face I had judged as that of a 25 year old began to change. Lines appeared in the brow. The cheeks sagged a bit, adding years to her countenance; yet, the jaw was set foreword, and the muscles in her neck were taut. I would swear that her hair had some gray streaks. This was now an angry, middle-aged woman I was facing. I found it difficult to breathe.)

She continued seemingly unaware of my distress. "As time passed, I finished the third and last book which will complete the series and assure my place in history. This new book is a story about the home front during the Second World War and includes the story of the death of the heroine in an air raid on a village, this village. It reads:" (She seemed to have it memorized.)

"The sound of a siren cut through the air. We ran from our house to the square. Lights were turned out, and the wardens with flashlights marked the way to the bomb shelter in the basement of the church. A number of bombs had already dropped in the lower section of the village, and houses were burning. Many of those streaming for the shelters had family in the lower village and were panicked at the sight of the flames and the sounds of the explosions. 'All this to get that witch,' one woman announced. Over one hundred villagers filled the basement hall of the church while others were hurrying into the basement of the nearby school.

The church basement hall was dimly lit, but they quickly recognized my mother. 'What is she doing here?' one of the women screamed.

'Get the witch out of here,' said another.

A third woman pushed my mother towards the door.

One of the wardens said, 'Here now, someone will get hurt!'

The husband of the first woman responded, 'My son and daughter haven't made it here. They are out in that blazing hell. We all know why they are bombing.'

'Bombing is evil. Witches are evil. They belong together,' cried another old crone.

They shoved my mother back out into the night and closed the heavy, steel shelter door. She was forced to seek shelter in the church, huddling by the entrance. Some moments later a bomb hit the church squarely, bringing the entire spire down on my mother.

Later, when the all clear sounded, and we left the shelter, we were welcomed by the sight of my mother's mangled body somehow disgorged from the rubble, lying not more than twenty feet from the basement bomb shelter entrance.

They cast her out and the bombing killed her!"

(She suddenly rose to her feet. Her chair upset and crashed to the floor behind her. Then, in what seemed to be a controlled rage, the now old woman continued through clenched teeth,)

"You see; I do remember! In fact, I never forgot. Now, with the story told and the manuscript at the publishers, their time is up. A storm is coming. A storm so huge that it will wash this entire God forsaken village and its vile people into the sea! I need to walk on the beach."

Conversation stopped at the bar. The door to the kitchen opened. The barman stepped out and followed her to the front door. He and the patrons silently watched her go. I left the food on the table, wedged through the gathering at the door and hurried to my car. As I drove up the long steep hill, I could see the storm clouds gathering.

CHAPTER SEVEN

Fifty years ago the Hebridians were dependent on the ocean for their food, employment and enjoyment. Most families fished one way or another, some for livelihood and others for supper. Boats, big and small, dotted the landscape. The tillable land was only a small acreage on each island, so the fish output paid for the import of a variety of food and other supplies. Considering the land mass dedicated to grazing, one would think wool would be the crop, but the grazing land was poor and limited the size of the herd. Still, some wool was exported, while the lamb provided variety for the table. One other item, barley produced scotch whisky for export, but the cost of the equipment limited the means of production to the wealthy. (We will hear more of the whisky business when we get to the Orkneys.)

The damp weather was both a curse and a blessing. The rotting of growth created the peat that heated the homes. The runoff provided the sheep with waterholes over the vast landscape and, in some areas, the crofters with water for washing and bathing. One beauty of wool is it stays warm even when wet. In addition, the lanolin sheds the water without absorbing it. It is the perfect cloth and yarn for these wet islands.

Unfortunately, most fruit trees and vines thrive on well-drained soil. Wet destroys metal equipment and rots fabrics. The storms make the fishing dangerous. Life in these islands is a challenge.

I was born and brought up on the seacoast of New England and was accustomed to the sea's idiosyncrasies. The wet weather was just one more thing that reminded me of home. Yet, there were beautiful summer days made for walking, taking a pack of rain gear just in case.

For the most part, the children of the isles were either in school, away on a larger island or the mainland, or they were helping with the business of the adults. But children, being what they are, one can imagine that they still found time to be children.

The Map

It all depends on how you look at it

The Isle of Lewis still had field-stone walled, thatch roofed *black houses* that were occupied until the mid 1900's. Scattered among these were quarried stone houses for the gentry. The house we are interested in was erected from quarried stone and was situated on the dunes above a sand cove. It was not an old house, not old by the isle's standards. Yet, it had seen its better days. It was Katie's family home.

The death of her husband in the war left Katie with two young children to care for and a small monthly dole payment too skimpy to pay the bills. While the children were on the mainland in school, Katie worked for the island clinic as a practical nurse. With this income and the dole payments, she somehow met the bills. It was a hard existence, but the people of the isles are a tough breed, and Katie was no exception.

Once the children were grown, she left the island and returned to school in Inverness to complete the required nursing courses to qualify and work there as a registered nurse. For a few years, summer vacations were opportunities to spend time with the family at the old homestead. As time passed, the children went their own way, and the island home became a luxury of little use. The property was rundown from years of poor maintenance and became a ruin. It finally reverted to the district for back taxes.

The rot of the roofing timbers and loss of slates let the rain trickle down the walls of the decaying house. Perhaps vandals, animals or just failure of the caulk, cracked and finally demolished the windows. The adhesive holding the wall-paper sheets disintegrated and the water-stained, faded paper peeled like a banana skin in uneven strips. These strips were caught by the wind blowing through the now glassless windows, torn into smaller sections, and carried off to parts unknown.

"What is it? Lemme see," ordered Jamie Finley. "Where did you get it?" Jamie was thirteen and realized that this was his last summer of freedom. His older brother had set the pattern, and Jamie knew that he would be expected to work his summer on the boat next year when he turned fourteen. The other three companions, his younger brother, his best friend and his cousin were *the gang*. Jamie was *the leader*.

Andy, his younger brother, was a good deal smaller than Jamie, but, as Scots are, feisty and not about to give up his treasure. "None of your business. I found it, and it's mine!" The other two boys knew how this was to end before it started. A wrestling match gave Jamie the advantage of weight and served the purpose much better than a fist fight since there would be no marks for Jamie to explain to his father later.

Jamie laid the irregular piece of paper, somewhat the worst for wear, on the hull of an old boat that had been upturned and beached for repair.

Jack, the third boy, unlike the two Finley brothers, was the quiet, brainy type. "It's a map," he said. This was instantly agreed to by the others since Jack had the role of oracle in *the gang*. "It's a treasure map," he then announced to the delight of the other three.

"Where is the treasure?" asked cousin Scully, wanting to believe Jack.

Jack pointed to a spot that at first looked like the imprint of a squashed bug. "It's here!"

"Which way is up?" asked Jamie, hoping the oracle could orient the map.

Jack just shrugged, then pointing to the outline that looked for all purposes like a watermark, he said, "We need to match this up with a shoreline, and that will tell us. There is a map of the island at MacGregor's. We could try to match up with that."

The four boys could hardly contain their excitement at the challenge of the quest. It wasn't the desire for riches but rather the promise of adventure that raised their spirits. They had visions of pirates digging in the sand by moonlight to conceal their booty from the authorities. Were the pirates hanged? Is that why they never came back to claim the treasure?

MacGregor's was a restaurant and pub, and the map was a dart board. It was lunch time, and there were a half dozen customers at the bar plus that many more eating lunch at tables in the adjacent room. The boys pushed their way through the door and more tumbled than ran past the bar into the side party room now open for darts. The board was hung from a hook on the wood panel wall which clearly showed the puncture wounds of poor marksmanship. The map scale was an inch to the mile so the plotted shoreline ignored all but the largest interstices. The boys' attempts to orient the treasure map soon drew a crowd. They were quickly dispossessed as the customers crowded in maneuvering the sheet this way and that trying to fit the dart board map's interpretation of the shoreline.

It proved to be a daunting task since the scale of the dart board map was obviously many times larger than the scale of the treasure map.

Finally, the dart board was put aside and common knowledge of the shore-line considered as to a fit with the seeming random configuration of the outline on the sheet. "That looks like...," and "This is certainly..." were pro-posed and discarded as ideas flowed in tandem with the ale. Still present, but now relegated to the periphery of the gathering, the boys were forgot-ten. Noonan, the proprietor, finally stepped in. "Settle down! Give me the sheet. We'll take it to Old Dogger. He used to jump everyone's pots and knows every inch of the island's shoreline."

The elevation of Old Dogger occurred just two years ago when the foul river rat called "*that dirty old dog*" by the local fishermen donated 100,000 pounds to the Mission for Homeless Fishermen. It turned out the *old dog* was rich. Automatically, his stature changed in the community, and he was carried along on the crest of the wave to respectability.

Age and liquor had taken their toll. The old man had given up his night sallies and now kept much to himself in a shed that had seen four genera-tions of his ancestors to their respective graves. Now, single and childless, his passing would allow the shack to collapse and be forgotten. It would hardly be worth scavenging from the remains. The building was a reflection of its owner. Veins stood out like cobwebs on his face, arms and legs. He seemed to be just flesh and bones, a scarecrow of a man. His voice was a dry rasp and his nose red and often runny as were his eyes. Yet, he still had that tough, unpredictable temper that had left him without friends and feared as a junk yard dog.

Taking the treasure map to Old Dogger was risky. The big worry was that Dogger, who chewed, would expectorate on the map, so they hauled up the spittoon and placed it to his left while the map was placed to the right on his kitchen table. "They's the Eilean Chaluim Chille," he said pointing, "and Loch Erisort. Doon you see it?" It took a moment for them to recognize the Island of Saint Columba from Dogger's imperfect Gaelic, but slowly, like a three-dimensional puzzle, they did see it! "They's noo road oot thar," Dogger concluded.

"What good's it do us on an island?" one customer asked Noonan.

Noonan countered, "There are five of us plus Dogger. We'll need a fair size dory."

"Noo problem, got it on wheels," said Dogger meaning his boat was on a trailer, "but I'm not rowin. You got it?" Dogger was above manual labor.

"My pickup has a hitch, sits three up front. The rest have to ride in the back," noted Noonan. "I'll close up for a day. We'll meet at the pub at six in the morning. Anyone late gets left, and I mean left out. First two get to ride in the cab." Now that was a big incentive to be early this time of year.

They left the pub the next morning at six on the nose. The boat was in the water by seven, and they were on the island by eight. The rowers were exhausted and dropped down on the shore. Neither Dogger nor Noonan took a turn in respect of their special positions. As the others recovered, Dogger oriented the map, and Noonan paced off a line on the shore to calibrate the map scale. Then, using Dogger's orientation, he paced off the distance from the shore to the treasure mark on the map. He ended up in the graveyard of the old ruined church.

Hauling up the pick axes and shovels from the dory, they all joined him and began to dig exploratory holes in the peat. They hadn't gotten far when a tall, skinny man with a hawk-like nose seemed to appear from nowhere. "What you fellers think yer doin?" he demanded.

Noonan spoke up. "What business is it of yours?"

"Perkins' my name. S my land you're digging on."

"Island's abandoned, ye damn fool," crabbed Dogger.

Perkins pointed at the main land, "S my house's over there. Island's my pasture."

That stopped the effort. "You might as well know; we're diggin for treasure. Got a map," Noonan showed Perkins the map.

"What's the boat for?" Perkins pointed to the dory.

"That's how we got here. Took a whole hour of rowin; no wind this early," Noonan said.

"See that," Perkins pointed. "Tha's a jetty so's you can drive across."

They all looked at Dogger. Not so smart after all, they thought.

To get things moving again, Noonan made an offer, "You can have an equal share if you dig with us."

"S wat's to keep me from gittin my shotgun an chasing yah off?"

"So, what do you want," asked Noonan?

"Half!"

More negotiation followed with Old Dogger settling the issue. "You know me, fool Perkins?" Perkins nodded. "Well, you mite chase us offn now, but I'll be back. You wants it that way?" Even share it was, and they resumed digging.

They dug holes all day and on into the evening. Bugs circling the lantern made shadowy images across the pitted landscape. As darkness replaced dusk, the diggers finally stopped. For what seemed an eternity, they rested and viewed the wreckage of their foraging. Finally, Perkins broke the silence, "Lemme see that map." He shone his flashlight on it for a moment and noticing a reflection from the back, turned it over. "Tha's paste chunks on the back. See!" He held up the sheet and shone the light on it. Then he turned it over and examined the 'map' side. "S nothin but stained wall paper."

They all looked and several spit on their fingers and ran them over the chunky residue. Tasting the smeared goo, they agreed. It was paste. The map was simply stained wall-paper!

Noonan swore them all to secrecy noting that they'd be the butt of jokes for years to come if the village found out. "We'll tell them we was fishin," and they all agreed.

Now Noonan wasn't one who took being made a fool of lightly. The next morning he asked the boys who found the 'map' to come in to the pub and made a big deal out of the find. He noted that he had talked to Old Dogger who identified the map as an outline of their own village cove. Handing it to Jamie, he pointed in the direction of the shore and wished them luck. You could see the shining light of expectation as Jamie said, "Really?'

"You bet," said Noonan.

After the boys left, there was a good deal of laughter from the five on-lookers, perhaps in relief that they weren't the only fools. In their minds, the boys deserved the pay back. After all, they started the dumb treasure hunt.

Stuart Stewart was the mail man who stopped at the pub on his rounds several days later. "Noonan, You heard about the boys' find, didn't you? Had an old map and fitted it up with the shoreline down the cove. The treasure point was in that nurse's old home, that abandoned ruin. The boys found a monstrance in a chest in the floor of the basement. Been there for centuries. Probably brought from France by Prince Jamie in '45."

"What's a monstrance?" asked Noonan.

"A sacred object. It is a cross with a large box for a base that holds the communion bread."

"Maybe those boys will want to start a church," mused Noonan. The onlookers laughed.

"Won't need to," remarked Stuart. "They could buy one. That Jacobite relic was worth fifty-thousand pounds to the jeweler in Stornoway. It was solid gold."

So, was it wallpaper, or was it a treasure map?

CHAPTER EIGHT

I had heard of the *singing sands* that were the basis for a Scottish detective story by Josephine Tey and hoped to see the phenomena first hand. I picked the Bay of Uig with its miles of dunes and sand basin as the place to explore. The problem was that it's located in the middle of nowhere.

The road through Glen Valtos, on the way in the driving rain, was an experience in itself. After hours of challenging driving, I reached a headland overlooking the bay. I stopped the car by a one-room school house that had been converted into a small museum and among all the clutter displayed, spotted a chess piece, not just any piece, a warder.

The Sands Of Uig

"On 17 October 1831, Frederic Madden, Assistant Keeper of Manuscripts in the British Museum, is said to have made the following entry in his journal, 'Sir Walter Scott came at two o'clock and stayed about an hour with me. I had the pleasure of looking over with him a set of very curious and ancient chessmen brought to the Museum this morning, for sale, by a dealer from Edinburgh named Forrest. They were discovered in a sand-bank on the west coast of Scotland, and are the most curious specimens of art I ever remember to have seen.'" (The Lewis Chessmen,"The Enigma of the Hoard," Neil Stratford, p.4.)

Even today we have very little knowledge regarding demons. 'Evil creatures' is a popular definition, a woefully inadequate description. "Who cares?" you might say. Well, you should, for these dark creatures are the source of every evil that inflicts mankind. They are the devil incarnate.

Now, you cannot become infected if you resist. Unfortunately, you may not realize you are at risk in time to fight back. Stealth is a demonic trade-mark. The demon master counts on this.

Oh, didn't I tell you about the demon master? Think of him as a rental agent or perhaps as a used car salesmen. He helps you to take a demon out for a spin, and if you like it, make it yours. And remember, this is done through stealth. You haven't a clue as to what you are getting. That is why it is an infection.

The Book of Times written late in the twelfth century tells the story of Magnus Ede, a dark cousin of Thorin, the Earl of Orkney.

The demon master in this case was Uris who used chess, a game of war, to deliver his gifts. He purchased fine walrus tusks and carved chessmen, kings, queens, warders, knights, and pawns.

"Warders?" you say. "What happened to the rooks?"

Well, this was the year Eleven Fifty, and those castles, the rooks that is, would not replace the warders for another hundred years.

So Uris charmed each of these pieces to be the conveyer of a demon. He made no special effort to link the type of piece to the type of demon. The choice was random. A king could host a simple hair demon that would turn the possessor of the piece bald. Another, a warder, could host a mind-robbing demon, the precursor to Alzheimer's. But, the large majority of the pieces were much more cataclysmic for warmonger, rapist and murderer were their charms. All you had to do was claim ownership and give the carving loving care. If you should realize the danger in time and give the piece away, the demon would go with it. But once infected, you became addicted and could no longer part with it. Many times individuals were targeted to receive a gift of a whole box of these horrors.

Now Magnus Ede had a long, successful career of plundering, or as it was now called, privateering. His annual horde from plundering was shared, as was the custom, with all those who might contribute to the success of his raids. First came his liege lord followed by his crew. Then came his confessor, his provisioner, the church, the shipwright, his mistress, his wife, four children, the taxman, and his mother-in-law. So, even in the best of times, Magnus found himself pressed for cash. He accepted a charter from Uris to act as his delivery agent.

Sailors, even pirates, are a superstitious lot. Magnus realized that his deal in the black arts had to be kept his secret. As captain and owner of the armed barque, he set the course and selected the ports of call for provisioning. There was plenty of time to make deliveries while the crew was on shore leave. And, best of all, he could keep all the payments to himself for only he and Uris would know of the moonlighting.

Uris' favorite targets were men of power. It was simple. He would wrap the chessmen in paper and place them in wooden boxes, one full set to each box. On the lid he would carve the name of the intended victim. Magnus would make the delivery.

Magnus made several trips to the continent to deliver a box to the Papacy and others to various kings. Finally Uris gave him a list of targets and half a dozen sets to take to the farthest reaches of the world. They were to sail beyond the Ice Lands and the Green Isles, to a far distant shore. There they would be given to the savage kings who would prosper in the evil power. Uris envisioned wars and the passing of the evil power to colonists who in turn would create an evil nation. The new world would be the great Satan in the west, "One nation, under Uris, with liberty and justice for none."

Magnus had never been west of the Northern Isles, but now that the destination was set, he was able to get a cargo consignment from local importers for the Ice Land to conceal his true assignment.

Once the hold was full, he sailed from Trondheim past Scapa Flow and the Orkneys and just north of Lewis. These were calm waters, and the crew had time to relax. The steward had seen the chess sets in the captain's cabin and, for some reason, seemed compelled to borrow one to play the bosun's mate. The game drew the interest of the whole crew with the exception of the officers who generally did not fraternize with the crewmembers. The captain and mate were busy plotting the course in the pilot house.

Thanks to the demons, the game turned ugly, and a brawl brought the officers in. They picked up the scattered board pieces to return them to the case only to find themselves choosing sides and joining the mayhem. Hearing the noise, Magnus and the Mate rushed to the main deck. There they were grabbed and thrown overboard. The brawl continued. Knives, pins and clubs took their toll until all were either dead or mad. The fresh winds of the North Sea caught the barque's full sail and drove the unmanned ship into the headland above Uig. Wreckage floated up on the sands and laid there in peace for over six hundred years.

My first visit to Uig was some fifty years ago. It proved to be frightening enough to keep me away for the next five decades. The island of Lewis had been caught in storms for a week before I arrived, and I bravely set off on a driving tour against the advice of the auto rental agent. In my ignorance, I picked the seaward shore as the first to explore. The very first day was to end in disaster.

I had been lost for well over an hour when I happened upon a church. I remember clearly that it had a bell hung on the outside wall facing the graveyard. The wind was force six, and the rain seemed to be falling horizontally. The windshield was fogged, and the air so humid that it defeated the defroster. Certainly, the church would offer a refuge from the storm. I slipped the poncho over my head and stepped out of the car. As I turned towards the church, a strong gust of wind forced me into the bonnet, and I slipped and fell. I thought I had left the car shut off, in gear and with the hand break on; yet, it rolled from the wind force just far enough to pin me under the front bumper. The pressure was sufficient to interfere with my breathing, and my struggle to pull free caused a sharp pain in my rib cage. The chilling rain water ran up the poncho, soaking my back, and the drops struck me in the face, blinding me. "Help," I yelled time and again until the combination of the wet and cold sapped my energy. It would soon be dark.

I had given up hope when I felt hands pulling on my hood and grabbing at my arms. In my delirium I saw the rescuers as wild dogs and tried to push them away. "Leave me alone," I cried out in my misery. The car was rolling again, but this time it was moving backward until I was pulled free. Then there was pain, sharp pain, as if someone were stabbing me. I tried to roll away from my tormenters, but they held me firmly. I blacked out.

I can't tell you how much time passed or even what day it was, but consciousness slowly, very slowly, came back to me. The first thing I saw was a kerosene lantern overhead and then faces above me asking me questions. It all sounded like gibberish. I pushed out with my arms to force them away, and the faces fled back into the darkness.

Next I awoke to a clacking sound and tried to sit up. The pain in my lower chest forced me back. Even as I lay still, the pain throbbed making me uncomfortable. In the glow of the oil lamp I could see a woman happily pedaling a loom with two shuttle cocks flying from side to side. Then she looked at me, and her expression changed to concern. She stopped the loom and came to my bedside to prop up my head and pour a dram of scotch into my mouth. It nearly choked me, but its warmth, as it traveled to my stomach, revived me allowing me to focus on my surroundings. "I need a doctor," I said, and marveled at the sound of my own voice.

My voice aroused others in the room, and they pressed in around the bed. The surrounding faces again spoke in gibberish. Who were these foreigners? Then my mind, which had been on a sabbatical, returned, and I realized that Gaelic was the mystery language.

"Does anyone speak English?" I asked. The word "English," caused a commotion, and now the faces were accompanied by hands gesturing and pointing in my direction. One face spat on the ground and repeated "English," with a vengeance.

The crowd moved away from me to the other end of the long, narrow room. They argued, pausing every so often to look over as if to see if I was listening. A very dirty looking, young girl bent over me and asked, "Are ye really English?"

"I'm an American," I answered.

"Is that in England?" she asked. She moved away as the crowd came back for another look. I pretended to be unconscious. Then, as if called forth by my play-acting, the fever came in a wave, and I truly lost consciousness.

Seemingly at a great distance, I heard a voice, a kind, caring voice, or perhaps the voice of my sickness, say, "It was the chess men."

I managed to say, "What?"

"The chess men," she repeated. "You must leave," she whispered quietly for my ears only.

"We need to dance," said another face that appeared behind her, and the sound of fiddle music filled the room. Now the faces had bodies. I seemed to be well again. I felt young. The bodies stepped around the bed twirling and, at the same time processing about the room. Around and around they went, and as they did, they grew younger. Then, as a daisy chain of young revelers, they went out the door.

Somehow I got to my feet thinking, *am I really doing this?* and followed them, twirling and prancing like the others. Then I realized that the weather had changed. The storm was gone. In fact, the ground was dry. I trailed after the procession as it wound down the track and out across the sands of the bay until suddenly it stopped. No more than ten feet from us a dead body of a man was lying against a sand mound. The dead man was clutching a small carved figure of a king, a chess piece. Bending over him was a poorly dressed peasant who must have been some local lord's gillie. He was picking chess men from the sand and stowing them in his bag. It was obvious from the splatter of blood on his tunic that he had killed the other man and was now stealing his treasure.

We took the thief by surprise. I could see the look on his face, at first defiant as he realized how young we were, and then fearful as he saw how many we were. Turning, he scrambled up the bank and fled across the dunes. He hadn't finished his work, and several dozen chess pieces remained scattered about in the sand. We quickly forgot about the murderer and completed the recovery of the chess pieces. I pocketed two.

Back at the village in the safety of the black house, we took the chess men out and hid them. We then told the story of the killing and escape of the gillie, not mentioning the chessmen. We left justice up to the adults.

Now, in an instant, I realized that at that time, I was one of the children. I lived in that village. I knew them all. I also understood the importance of the chess pieces. Don't ask me how; I just knew.

Bad boys, the Murchison twins were always fighting. Say the wrong word and Erin Murchison would make you eat it. Lyle was quiet but carried the same chip on his shoulder. He would wait his chance and then strike when you didn't expect it. He nearly killed Tom Mhore for nothing at all. Tommie was a big boy, too. The teachers feared the Murchison boys, and they had good reason. And now those boys controlled demons, or the demons controlled them.

Maureen MacLeod ate flies. She would now have to increase her intake to feed the demons as well as herself.

Ann Mhore had always thought of herself as a young witch. Her father indentured her to a merchant man as a servant. She murdered him when he tried to rape her in her sleep. Then she returned home. She knew evil before she took the chess pieces.

There were a dozen children in all. I knew every one.

Returning from my fevered memories to consciousness in the room of my confinement, I slowly rolled to the edge of the bed. Every move produced a sharp pain in my chest. The kind woman wrapped a shawl around my back. I realized I had nothing else on except a nightshirt. Seeing that I was finally awake and mentally alert, she helped me up and, positioning the shawl over my shoulders, guided me to the door. The wind was still blowing, and the rain stung as it hit my face as we made our way up the lane. "I can't make it," I said, but the woman would have none of it.

"You must," she answered and nearly dragged me up the lane.

In just a few yards the rain had soaked me, and the chill sent painful shudders through my chest. My stomach was sick, and I felt like vomiting, but the thought of the pain that would bring, forced me to hold back.

There was my car, not twenty yards from the old church. "The keys, I don't have the keys," I rasped. She pulled open the door, and I saw that they were in the ignition. If I could just get in. It seemed like an eternity. First I sat, backing into the driver's seat. She bent over and picked up my legs and lifted them in. Each one weighed a ton. The car was in gear with the brake on. I pushed in the clutch, turned the key, and it started.

I couldn't get the brake to release!

The others were coming. They heard the car start. The woman shut the door and hurried out of sight. I could not pull upwards with sufficient force to release the brake. Each time I tried the pain was like a knife in my chest. The brake was set and locked.

They were here. I pressed the horn and for a moment that stopped them. I used that moment of hesitation to lock the doors. Finally, out of frustration I brought my knee up hard, and it lifted the brake handle. The handle snapped to the release position.

I would run them down! I pressed hard on the gas. The car shot backwards up the lane, throwing me against the wheel. I had it in reverse instead of first. Then the car stalled. The pain was so sharp I began to lose consciousness.

My window smashed, showering glass over me. Hands grabbed at the shawl, and I let go of it. I tried to restart, but the hands found the door lock and pulled the door open. As I fought to turn the ignition key, they pulled me from the car. I reached into the pocket of the nightshirt and grasped the two objects I had kept with me, the chess pieces.

The next moment I found myself on the ground in the glare of the headlights. My pants and shirt were soaked under the poncho. I could feel the pain in my ribs from the pressure of the bumper of the car where it had pinned me. Now the car had been pushed back off me. The people standing by helped me sit up. "Broken a rib, I bet, lad," the man holding my arm said.

They helped me to my feet and offered shelter in their village. My mind raced through the dreams or delusions trying to understand what had happened. I needed time to sort it out. "No, I'm fine," I lied and moved to get into the car. No broken window, no nightshirt, no wet seat, I needed time to understand this. I slowly backed the car up the lane and into the churchyard. There I turned and then drove away.

Now, fifty years later, as I sat in a rental car and looked over the bay, I realized why the sight astonished me. The sands of Uig, shining yellow in the sunlight, stretched for miles along the shore and back into the bay, a giant sand shingle.

Things had changed; the road, then a wagon path, was now paved. The thatched *black* houses were gone. Road signs pointed the direction to the village, and a proper museum had been opened in an old hall in place of the schoolhouse, commemorating the Gaelic history of the area.

The people in the museum told me that only one resident, Mary MacLeod, remained from the 1950's. They said that Mary is the great-granddaughter of Malcolm, the first owner of record of the Lewis Chessmen. She is ninety-three years old. They directed me to her small croft house overlooking the harbor.

I knocked, and a woman with dull gray eyes and a wrinkled face opened the door. Her house dress was long, touching her ankles, and showed the fading that always accompanied too many washings. "Mary MacLeod?" I asked.

"What business have you with Mary?" she asked. "I'm her sister."

"Tell her it is about the chessmen," I answered.

"Come," she said without further question and went down the hall to the back door. I followed. She held the door open for me, and as I walked out onto a small stoop, I saw a face I recognized. It was older now but still had the same expression of concern, the look of kindness that I had seen fifty years before.

"It has been a long time," Mary said. "I thought you had forgotten."

I couldn't wait for pleasantries. "The children, Mary. What happened to the children?"

"The clearances," she answered. "They wanted our land for grazing. The children went to Australia, New Zealand, South Africa, and India."

"The chess pieces, I responded?"

"Went with them," said Mary.

"Why was I there," Mary?

"And finally to the new world with you, the United States of Uris," she added.

The two objects from my nightshirt? They're here, my king and queen.

CHAPTER NINE

From Thurso in the north of Scotland I took the P & O ferry further north to Stromness on Mainland Orkney. Fifty years ago the tourist industry had not discovered this wonderland of ancient ruins. Scara Brae, the Stone-Age village, was still a curiosity in a cow pasture. Maes Howe tomb was a bump in a very bumpy landscape reached by following a dirt path through a field. It was late in the day when I arrived at the Howe, a large dirt mound covering an ancient burial chamber. My hope was to find the wall carving that the Norse invaders had left when they broke in through the roof of the tomb. This carving, called the Maes Howe Dragon, was only the size of a silver dollar. The long squat entranceway was dark and damp. Inside I was alone. While I was using a flashlight to hunt for the scratched-in Dragon, two huge women struggled through the tunnel opening carrying a sizable beam light. The sudden, intense light momentarily blinded me. The beam played all over the walls until it stopped on a bit of Runic graffiti.

"Look at this, my dear," walrus number one said.

"Oh, it is one of those magical writings most likely putting a curse on everyone who enters," said walrus number two.

"Then we must leave at once," said walrus one, and they hurried out.

The writings they illuminated were graffiti such as, "You should try ...... in the village." The Vikings who raided these tombs in the Ninth Century and scratched the Runes on the walls were a lusty lot.

Another howe I visited, the Unstan Tomb had contained Unstan pottery indicating that the ancients traded with the mainland prehistorics to the south. To explore Unstan Tomb it was necessary to ask permission to enter the sheep-filled pasture surrounding the tomb. A sign directed one to a nearby farmhouse to ask for the gate key. As a way of repaying the farm woman for the opportunity to trespass, I bought several of the black and white picture postcards she was selling.

Today these ruins have been commercialized, and tourists, by the flock, like geese, have stolen their charm. So many rubbings have been made of the dragon that the actual etching is nearly rubbed out.

Fifty years ago, these remote isles were still magical. The walrus was right about that. The people living in the Orkneys were still untainted by the modern world. For example, when asked if she had been abroad, Mrs. Johnston who ran a guest house in Stromness replied, "Of course. I've been to Rousay." Rousay is a small island several miles away from Mainland Orkney.

Force six winds and driving rain on the day of my arrival in Stromness and for several days after made this ancient Viking town seem like the end of the earth. I biked out to the Standing Stones of Stenness in this fury and was so exhausted that I sheltered in the lee of one of the stones. As I stood there, a Mercedes pulled up, a chauffer got out and opened the door for a man in a long, cashmere coat. The man pulled out a camera and told me in snotty-toned English to get out of the way. He snapped a picture, got back in, and the Mercedes drove off to his next ancient artifact leaving me standing in the pouring rain. One can see why the Scots might loathe the English tourists.

For the next several weeks of exploring, those two interruptions were my only encounter with tourists. I, of course, was not a tourist. I was a storyteller. I was at home in Stromness for it reminded me of my own childhood on the ocean: the trawlers moving in and out and unloading fish, the gulls screeching overhead, even the squall weather seemed to be old friends. I slept well and dreamed of a *red-haired girl.*

The Red-Haired Girl

Knowledge has a price

For thousands of years men have been fishing with nets, some by throwing them over the side and hauling them in, and others by fixing them to the bottom and snagging the passing fish in the netting. With the advent of power boats, trawling, that is dragging nets weighted to the bottom, became the common commercial method. These fishermen were often called *draggermen*. The smaller trawlers, common in the Western Isles and Orkney, had a crew of four and a capacity of up to fifty tons of fish storage in the hold on ice. The average fishing voyage was seven days at sea, five days of that fishing.

Part One James' Story

The fishing, north and west of Scotland, was generally good, but the catch depended on the captain's ability to find the fish. Fish migration patterns were seasonal, depending on water currents and temperatures which were influenced by the weather. The patterns repeated year after year so the knowledgeable captains with well-kept records could anticipate the migration and locate the fish. Yet, at times, for no seemingly good reason, after years of repetition, the migration pattern would suddenly change for that year, defying the charts and turning voyages into scouting missions. Foreclosures were common in bad years since most boat owners had mortgage payments to meet requiring a steady flow of saleable product. This impacted the fishermen crew as well as the boat owners since the crew worked for a percentage of the take, after expenses. Poor catch, poor pay.

It was then a few years after the end of the Second World War, before ultrasonic fish detection, catcher boats, and factory ships common today. Young *draggerman* deck hand James MacLean was coming up the Stromness dock, tired and dispirited from a disappointing week at sea. The catch would barely cover expenses, leaving little or nothing for the crew. James' father owned a share in another boat so some money was available for the family, but James had a special need for money. He wanted to buy his own boat.

As he approached the pier, he noticed a girl or perhaps a young lady, a very beautiful young lady, moving to intercept him. She stopped in his path and stood for a moment as if to catch her breath. When she spoke, it was a quiet statement, almost a whisper, "I ken where the fish are," she said in a confiding tone.

Moving to pass her James responded, "I ken where they aren't, lass!"

Perhaps it was the long, red hair, her fine features, the excitement in her eyes or maybe his shame at the rudeness of his response to her statement that caused him to turn and stare. It was foolish to think that this snip of a girl could know something that the best of the captains in the port could only guess at. Yet, she was so pretty that it took his breath away. He had to stop and turn, and now he needed to say something or feel the fool. "Where?" he finally asked.

"Tomorrow go out past Graemsay on the leeward towards Cava. Fish from the light of Graemsay on through the Deeps." Then she added, as if worried he would pay no heed, "Will ye do it?"

"It's not my boat, lass," James responded, "but I'll try."

Then, as if embarrassed by her own actions, the girl turned and rushed back up the pier, past the Fisherman's Inn, up John's Street, and out of sight. For a moment she was there, and then she was gone, but James would not forget her. Stromness was a small town. He had not seen her before. She must be new or perhaps visiting, he reasoned. *I did na even ask her name,* he thought. *How could I let her run off like that?* Finally, the exhaustion of seven days at sea caught up with him, and he headed for his home.

Boats do not make money tied to the dock. In a bad year, when the catches were small, the trips had to be more frequent. James returned to the ship the very next morning at five for the next voyage. *How could she know?* he reasoned over and over to himself. Yet, coming on board, he went straight to the captain and told him he had a request. He asked if they could set the trawl in the trough that ran from Graemsay to Cava on the way out to the fishing grounds.

The captain would have laughed at the suggestion of fish in that close to the ferry channel but, wanting to keep a hard worker like James on the crew, decided to humor him. Once they had passed Greamsay, they lowered the net, attached the doors, and reeled out the cables until the net bottomed.

The trawler slowed from seven to three knots from the weight of the drag and then suddenly to a standstill as the net snagged.

"Some old wreck on the bottom," griped the captain. "This will probably tear the net. I was foolish to set the trawl so near Stromness."

The crew began the task of recovering the net. The boat was reversed, and the cables were winched in slowly to pick up the slack. After recovering the slack from the reverse movement of the boat, the winch labored as it attempted to lift the net and recapture the doors. The boat shifted under the strain. "We must have part of a wreck caught in the net," the Captain shouted over the groan of the winch.

As the net came out of the water, they were struck by an unbelievable sight. It was bursting with fish. They were unable to hoist the cod end and had to dump the net in sections to allow the hoist to lift such a heavy load. It normally took hours of trawling to even partially fill the net. In minutes on this trawl, they had filled it to overflowing.

When the net had been completely emptied, nearly two tons of fish were piled on the deck. Time and again the trawl was set, and each time the net refilled before they were able to clean and pack the catch from the previous full net. They worked all day and through the night and were in port the next morning to unload the best catch of the season.

Who was she, and how did she know? James thought. The very next morning he went looking for her, but no one at the fish dock knew her. "Is there a new family in town?" he then asked.

"There is a new ferry master," one of the lumpers on the dock answered.

James rushed to the ferry dock where the stevedores pointed out a stone building down the harbor about two miles telling him to ask for Mary. "Mary, Mary, beautiful Mary, quite contrary," James muttered under his breath as he hurried to the ferry master's home. "Where's Mary?" he shouted to the children playing in the yard, and they pointed out on the moor. He saw her staking a goat and walked briskly to her side.

"How did you ken, lass?" he asked, but she said nothing. "I've ne'r seen so many fish," he added. But still she said nothing. "Oh," he said, finally becoming aware that he had failed to introduce himself. "I'm James MacLean."

"I ken," said Mary, and then realizing that this showed more interest than she wanted to admit, she blushed. James found himself unable to think of something to say. She was an angel dropped from heaven in his eyes. What could he say that would interest so lordly a person?

"Are you gaein' to the dance tonight?" he asked lamely.

"I thought about it, but I do na ken anyone and would feel uncomfortable to go there and back alone," she noted.

"I'll walk you there and back if you will dance with me," James said wanting to add *only* but feared to make any demand that might chase her away. She nodded approval. Again there was that pause as two shy souls tried to find a topic to prolong the interview. It was James that spoke first. "Do you ken where the fish will be in two days?" he blurted out. Immediately, he wished he had not said it, realizing that she would think his interest was in the fish only. "Ay, it's not that important," he said quickly, trying to offset her obvious disappointment.

"Perhaps I'll know by tonight," she answered.

Again they stood, each unable to think of the hundreds of questions they could naturally ask to get to know one another. Again it was James that spoke, "I'm sorry I have no horse, but I'll be here at dusk to walk you to the dance." Then embarrassed by his lack of meaningful small talk, and yet finding it difficult to leave her, he turned back to the road for the two mile walk home. He didn't see her wave.

That evening everyone wanted to dance with the new red-haired beauty, and yet she managed to dance with James the majority of the sets. He was walking on air. It almost seemed like magic. She was all he could see or think about. And she did tell him where the fish would be.

This time it took the boat the better part of the day to get to the place Mary had described. James simply told the captain that he had a premonition as to the location. They set the trawl at first light, and by day's end had nearly filled the hold. Bad weather drove them back in before they were able to complete the trawl, but they still had the second best catch of the season.

Time and time again Mary's predictions proved to be correct, and the only misses were those cases where James had misunderstood her description of the location. Yes, he saw her every day he was on shore. Yes, she predicted the location of the fish. But that was a small part of a new and wonderful period in their lives. Love filled every moment of their meetings.

Mid-summer they were married, and James told her of his plan to own his own boat, now with Mary's help.

However, there were things that puzzled James. Mary insisted they rent a cottage near her parent's home nearly two miles from town. In addition, before she would make a prediction as to the location of the fish, she always took a walk on the moor. She cautioned him not to follow her, or there would be no prediction. Once he tried, and she made her point by turning back and refusing to locate the fish.

Mary didn't know the coast of Orkney and the surrounding waters. She was from the Western Isles. Her descriptions were difficult to place and seemed to be more so as time went on. "Off Hascosay in the sound," said Mary. But which sound, Hascosay Sound, South Sound or Colgrave? When James asked questions to help locate the place, she had to walk on the moor again to answer the questions. It seemed as if it took longer on the moor as time went on, and at the same time the answers became less helpful. Could she be intentionally misleading him? The walks on the moor, could she be a witch?

Even with the misdirection, the times James' locations were correct made his trawler the most profitable in the harbor. Yet, James yearned for his own ship which would take an increase in the frequency of the huge catches. With this on his mind he tended to count the misses rather than the hits. He tried to make Mary understand. Could she improve the prediction if he gave her a map, or could he please walk on the moor with her to ask the questions and shorten the response time? It had now begun to take so long to get answers that Mary was away more than she was home.

What or who was on the moor?

Then one day they had their first argument. He felt that Mary simply could not understand his impatience, and she insisted she could not improve her prediction accuracy. Both were frustrated to the point that James became angry. Mary had no response and fled to the moor in tears.

When she didn't return by dark, James went out looking for her. As the evening drew on, he asked her family for help, admitting his ill temper and her tearful escape. The search went on for days with James calling on more and more island people to help. No trace of her was found.

Some said she had taken the steamship to Thurso on the mainland and others that she had killed herself. Still others said James may have done something with her. All blamed James for her flight, and James himself agreed. After some months of looking, realizing she was not going to re-turn, James went to work on the oil rigs in the North Sea never to return to Orkney.

Part Two Mary's Story

Mary was the child of John Murchison of Lewis and Ann Johnson of Shet-land, Ann having met Murchison when he was a young officer for the P&O. Mary was their oldest daughter, a quiet girl whose first interest on arriving at her new home on Mainland, Orkney was to walk on the moor and wonder at the beauty of the seascape. From the moor Mary could see Hoy, Graemsay and in the distance, Scapa Flow. It was so different from her home on Lewis. Although she would miss her friends in Stornoway, she had always been a bit of a loner and rejoiced at the prospect of discovering a new island and a new city, Stromness.

A stop at a deep, dark, spring-fed pool provided her first contact on the island for as she dipped her hands into the water to cool her face, another older woman with long, red hair stared back. More from reflex action than thought Mary blurted out, "Who are you?"

"I'm called the Lady in the Pool, Mary. I'm here for you."

"I do na ken," said Mary, but there was no answer. "How did ye get thar?" That and many other personal questions went unanswered. It was only when Mary shifted the questions to the landscape of the island that the lady began to respond. She told Mary of the Ring of Brodgar, the Stones of Stenness, the prehistoric tombs of Maes Howe and Unstan. Each had a story, and Mary listened in rapture. There was so much to see and do. And now she had her own confidant.

From that time on, Mary spent a bit of each morning at the pool visiting with her new friend.

The vision cautioned her not to tell of their meetings nor allow others to follow her to the pool, or the Lady would have to stop meeting with Mary. "I'm here for you, Mary, and you only," the Lady said.

One day while running her mother's errands in town, Mary passed by the dock. A fisherman caught her eye. He was a young lad, not much older than she was. His sandy hair was sun-bleached almost blond, and he was deeply tanned. He stood tall and straight from hard work but had a kind face and smiling eyes. She began to watch for him around town and soon learned that his name was James MacLean. "How can I meet him?" she asked the lady in the pool.

"Tell him you know where the fish are," the Lady answered.

"But I don't know where the fish are."

"I will tell you," the Lady assured her. So Mary met James, and the fish predictions came true.

Was it love or his need to find the fish? Whatever, she felt a bond grow between them. As time went on and they were married, she realized that her predictions were getting less accurate. Oh, the fish were at the spot the lady said they were, but the description was often incomplete, or so it seemed. In addition the lady was taking longer to appear each time Mary came to the pool. Many times the Lady's answers to James' questions seemed misleading, and this caused friction in their marriage. Once James had followed her out onto the moor, but cover was sparse, and she spotted him before she arrived at the pool. She walked him back to their cottage and had, of course, no information to give him. She didn't dare to go back out that day for fear he would follow again.

"Why can't I have James come and ask you directly about the place to fish? He knows the ocean, and I don't," pleaded Mary.

"No, you must not let him come here. I'm here for you, Mary," the Lady emphatically insisted.

"James is so intent on owning his own boat. If only I could guide him to the fish each time, he'd have enough money for the down payment this fall to convince the bank to loan him the rest. Even if the bank would not make the loan, others would buy shares. James said so. With the poor season, there are a number of boats for sale at a good price. Now is the time. We can't wait until the fishing improves for everybody. There won't be a boat to be had. What should I do?" asked Mary.

The Lady was silent.

Then one day came the argument with James. Mary couldn't make him understand. If she told him of the Lady, the Lady would be gone, and there would be no more fish advice. But as it was, he was clearly frustrated and beginning to think she was intentionally misleading him. Then again, was the Lady in the pool misleading her? Why should she? What reason could she have? They were friends, weren't they? "She knows everything," Mary thought. "If only I had that knowledge..."

At the pool in tears, having run from James' anger, she told the Lady of her frustration. "If I only had your knowledge. If I were like you," Mary pleaded as she stood by the pool.

"What do you wish, Mary?" the Lady asked.

"I wish I were like you," cried Mary without thinking.

Can you step through a mirror? Now, from experience, I'd say "no," but at that moment, by some evil magic associated with that dark pool, Mary took the Lady's place, deep in its chilled waters.

"Now, you must seek a red-haired girl. You will be here for her, Mary," the departing voice explained.

CHAPTER TEN

In writing the story of the Red-Haired Girl I assumed that the channel out of Stromness past Hoy and Greamsay was capable of being trawled. That is, that it was clear but not too deep. Seeing the large P & O steamer come down the length of the channel made me question my judgment so I took the evening work ferry, a converted trawler, on the round trip to the two islands to drop off islanders that worked in Stromness. I would survey the waterway myself.

The Lady in the Peat

To Betty Corrigall, the true "Lady of Hoy"

I met him while standing at the rail of the small ferry from Stromness to Hoy in the Orkneys, an island group north of Scotland. He was a man of middle-age, average height, heavy set, dark hair and ruddy complexion, someone who had obviously made his life in the open. I guessed that he was a fisherman out of Stromness on his way to his home on Hoy. I didn't pry.

Now that doesn't mean I didn't ask questions. As usual, I explained my interest in the stories of the islands and in particular of the *Old Man of Hoy*, a monolith off the magnificent Hoy cliffs facing Graemsay. He responded in a friendly manner that he would like to be helpful but simply considered it a "big stack." When I asked him about the channel we were traveling in, he became expansive but was cut off by his companion.

His mate, a frail lass who stepped between us, suggested I consider "The Lady" instead of a pile of rock. The interruption caught me off balance. She was so plain and wan looking that I had hardly noticed her. My first instinct was to turn away back to the *fisherman*, but she was not so easily put off. She had a story to tell, and I was to be her audience.

And now you are the audience.

Yet, before I turn her loose on you, I think it would help if you had a short primer on sin. So this story really begins in Leviticus, Chapter twenty-six. In summary God said:

> "If you reject my laws and my customs, you will suffer terror, consumption, and fever. Your foes will defeat you. If you still fail to follow them, the sky will become like iron, and the soil like bronze. Your crops will fail. And if still you continue, I will send wild animals to attack you and steal your children, destroy your cattle and reduce your numbers until the roads are deserted. And if you still will not, I will take your bread and set your enemies on you. You will have pestilence in your towns. And if you still go on, you will eat the flesh of your own sons and daughters. I will reduce your lands to deserts and towns to ruins. And the few that are left will have such fear that the sound of a falling leaf will strike terror in their hearts."

And so believed the Elders of the Scottish Church.

The year is seventeen seventy, the '45 is still in the minds of the populace, and the clearances have begun. Already the land has been divided among those lords and masters who supported Gloucester. The crofters, lease holders and freemen have been reduced to a life of poverty matching slavery. The farms have been combined into large estates and independent farming discouraged to make room for sheep pasture. Farmhands and small land holders are forced to turn to fishing or to "removal" to other shores.

The so-called parish church is a chapel of the lord of the land and the pastor his employee. Since the church officials are paid by the estate owners, they often side with these masters against the common people. Like petty tyrants, these owners cherish their superiority to the commoner and dispense "God's justice" with a heavy hand.

Here in the islands the common folk have but two choices; they either farm or fish, and both mean servitude since the lands and the boats are owned by the gentry. The tenants, crofters, peasants, servants, gillies, tacksmen and such as have not left for foreign shores, are allowed to sit in the church, well to the rear of the lord and his family, separated from them, by a screen.

Attendance is required, for the lord considers his inferiors to be sinners needing forgiveness. Why else are they in such lowly state if they are not put there by God as punishment?

After the Sunday service, the lord of the manor, guided by the cleric, dispenses justice and also small gifts for special services. Millie has often received these tokens for her devotion to her mistress, the lord's wife. With Millie's position comes grave responsibility, for Millie must be wed to her job, living only for the comfort of the grand dame. Much as the Egyptian queens had castrated their male servants, Millie must remain unwed and place her mistress first, last and always.

Craggie House was built in the fourteen hundreds, and although altered and expanded by the Morrisons, the main building, the two-story manse that forms the center of the edifice, remains as the original construction. The manse stands on a small knob that gives it a view across Morrison land as far as the island's high cliffs. The estate is so large that it takes a full day to walk around it.

Second only to the lord, the lady runs the house. Counting the grounds keepers, there are some twenty-three servants in the household. Some do the cooking, others the cleaning, and still more the wash. These all live in the village about a mile from the manor. Millie, however, lives in Craggie House and has a room adjacent to her mistress. The other servants are required to treat Millie with deference as they would a member of the family.

Hers is a life-long position with good shelter, the best food, room service, and many other perks because of her proximity to the mistress of the house. She is considered her mistress' companion, and so she has to dress the part. Her wardrobe is full of both social and sporting attire provided by her ladyship. She is her lady's spokesman to the rest of the servants, speaking with authority of proximity to the seat of power. Many a starving peasant would have considered Millie's situation heaven itself.

But in the real world, even in seventeen seventy, girls will be girls. Millie has a secret boy friend.

Now, before you condemn Millie for her behavior, you should realize that marriages are often arranged. That is one reason for the addition of "wings" on Craggie House. The lady's bedroom is far from the lord's and, never in memory, visited by his lordship. However, others did visit her ladyship so she set the tone for indiscretion, allowing her servant the same freedom to entertain so long as this did not hinder Millie in her service to her ladyship.

There are a number of other families in the town besides the servants to the Manse. The several large estates on the island require considerable provisioning, and in return, sell large quantities of wool to the mills in Pitlochry. Agents for the provisioners and the mills have to be accommodated when they visit so there is an inn. In addition, the townspeople require goods and have handicrafts to sell, adding commercial service people to the village population. Finally, there are families that simply live in the village because it is their home. Among these are the Grays.

The Gray males have always been seamen. On land these men folk are fish out of water. There are seven Gray children, four brothers and three sisters. The boys of the Gray family leave for sea at fifteen continuing a family tradition that goes back centuries. Wilson Gray is twenty four, tall and thin, with the family's red hair and freckles. Like all the other Grays he comes to land only to spawn. There is no end of red-haired and freckled children among the populace stemming from this habit. Unfortunately, Wilson finally meets Millie.

By the time Millie realizes she is pregnant, Wilson is off on a nine month whaling run, not that he would have done the proper thing anyway. Now, in these times of male dominance, the man is blameless, and the pregnant woman cast out as an example of sinfulness. The good pastor would champion the process, even pointing her out from the pulpit as a common tramp. He would recite the curse and evoke heavenly punishment on her, an example to his parishioners of the power of his position as God's chosen. All the "good" Christians would shun her, and her family would be shamed.

Why d'ya na leave me alone! Millie thinks in sadness. But they won't, and she knows it. There is no choice. She has to kill herself.

Now, if this decision is the end, there would be no story, but alive or dead, Millie has just started her performance on the stage of planet Earth

Dusk is a time for ghosts and ghouls to rise from the graves, and dawn is the time for their return. Challenging the natural flow of the spirit world, Millie unfortunately chooses dusk to drown herself. Making no attempt to swim, she walks into the sea. As the breakers wash over her, she feels hands grabbing her, pulling her into a dory. A passing lobsterman returning from his run sees her being swallowed by the surf and comes to her rescue. "Millie girl," he scolds. "What is in your mind, walking in the surf with an outgoing tide? You could have been killed!"

Millie, spitting sea water and plucking kelp from her hair, can't contain her frustration. "Why d'ya na leave me alone!" she sputters.

Once you turn Death loose, it becomes a relentless spirit.

Late the next afternoon, after a busy day with her lady, Millie again considers her fate. *Jump from a cliff*, she decides. Hoy has so many high and dangerous heights. A fall to the beach below and then swept away to a grave in the surf, no questions asked, no rescue from drowning; it is a perfect plan.

One of the highest cliffs on the island is only a mile from the house. She wraps herself in a heavy wool cloak and puts a kerchief over her head. Must not catch cold, she thinks.

At the cliff, she gingerly steps to the edge, and looks down on the rocky shore below. "Jump," she tells her legs. "Jump," she commands, but somehow a little voice in her mind says, "It is cold and wet down there." Just yesterday she had walked into the surf. What is wrong now? I'm afraid of heights, she realizes. She shivers and steps back.

"Now, Millie girl," she mutters, "you haven't walked all this distance to fail again. Pull yourself together." These are brave thoughts, and she congratulates herself silently for her stubbornness.

Again, summoning all her courage, she approaches the edge. She is sure she can do it this time, but that thought is interrupted by the reproach, "Be careful, you foolish girl. A gust of wind could topple you over, and you would be cut to pieces on the rocks." A tall gaunt man is approaching.

"Cut to pieces!" exclaims Millie as she turns to face the old school master. She had counted on a quick, painless end. The moment has passed; her courage is gone. She can't face the thought of pain. "Why d' ya na leave me alone!" she sulks.

On her way back to the house, she finally thinks of the fool-proof solution. She stops at the estate's barn, goes in and bars the door. "No intruders this time," she mumbles. She places a barrel under a high beam. The barn is a good forty feet high, and the beams are at least twenty-five feet from the floor. Throwing a rope over a beam, she ties one end to the horse stall. She stands on the barrel and fashions the other end into a hangman's noose. She places it over her head and under her chin. Without a moment's hesitation and before common sense can step in to stop her, Millie kicks the barrel out from under her feet. She drops like a stone until the slack is gone, and the rope snatches her like a fish hooked in a stream.

At this point, I know you expect the rope to break, and perhaps it does; for next she finds herself sitting in an open box surrounded by dozens of frightened people.

Seeing the hanging and resurrection from Millie's frame of view has caused us to overlook nearly two hundred years of elapsed time. To remedy this, we must leave the frightened throng and turn back to the estate barn and the time of the hanging.

The next morning, intent on mucking out the stalls, a stable boy finds the body. The lord is called, and Millie is cut down. The carpenter constructs a box, but before Millie is placed in it she must be redressed. The clothing she has on belongs to her lady. So Millie is dressed by the servants in a castoff dress. Finally, she is placed in the box, and the lid is nailed in place.

The coroner is local and convenes an adhoc hearing on the spot. The verdict is suicide, and so Millie's plight takes on a whole new shame, one Millie did not foresee.

The box is loaded onto the burial wagon, pulled by a half-starved horse, driven by the world's oldest mortician, and taken to the church for burial. Naturally, the churchman is informed for death is a state in eternal life. Unfortunately, suicide is a sin, the work of Satan, and this pastor is a sworn enemy of the devil. "No service," he proclaims from the pulpit, and "No burial in consecrated ground for this child of Satan." So Millie escapes from one shaming condemnation and falls right into another. "Take her body back to his lordship. She was his servant."

The burial wagon returns to the estate. His lordship is even less hospitable than the pastor, if that is possible, and refuses to accept the body. "She came to work here from Mowat's. Let them do with her." Again the body is sent by wagon, this time across the estate boundary to the next district.

Mowat's has no burial ground and sends the wagon back to Craggie House.

To settle the impasse, the lords of the two estates finally agree to place the box in a peat bog about fifty yards off the main road at the boundary line between their properties. The box is dug into the bog, covered with soggy, peaty soil, with no marker, and forgotten for over one hundred and fifty years.

One of the treasures of the Scottish islands is the huge layer of peat that covers their moorlands. This peat, cut and dried, resembles soft coal, without its sulfurous emissions. It is ideal for burning in shallow fireplaces to take the chill and damp off the misty mornings. About five tons of peat, cut and dried, provide one ton of fuel. The larger bogs are apportioned to the various families in the area so that cutting will be orderly.

The year is now nineteen thirty-seven. It is a cold, dark, damp, fall day. The wind is blowing, and a fine mist rolls over the island. These weather patterns come and go, sometimes changing two or three times a day, but this one has lingered for the better part of three days. At misty times like this it is hard to navigate, so the fishermen are land-bound. This gives them the chance to catch up on family chores postponed for the "rainy day."

One such family, the Allan's, is cutting and stacking peat in their allotment, when William, the youngest son, strikes a wooden object buried about two feet down in the peat. One of the remarkable things about the peat is its power to preserve. The wood does not crumble when the spade strikes it. It is as resilient as the day it was placed in the bog. Charlie, the Allan's oldest boy, digs down one edge of the wood surface exposing the side of a box. The third brother, Peter, with the help of several flat stones to jack against, uses his shovel to pry the box upward out of the peat. He then edges it over, away from the hole.

Rain begins to fall as a North Sea storm approaches, but the small family gathering hardly seems to notice. The Allan family crowds around to stare at the box. Is it a treasure? Finally, Alex, the father, sends Willie back to the village to get the postmaster who is the village's only uniformed official and, as such, the authority on all matters. Willie rides to the village on his bike rather than taking the tractor since the bike is much faster. Dark clouds, thunderheads, form overhead as the mist and light rain turn into a wind-driven downpour.

The post office is in the general store, and Willie finds it crowded with people shopping for supplies before the storm moves in. "Postmaster," he says, "we dug up a box in the peat bog. Might be treasure. Come; see." The shopping ends instantly. The shoppers spill out of the store and head for the bog.

Now to comprehend the excitement of the villagers you need to understand that the isle of Hoy is truly a remote place. People are born here, they live here, and they die here, perhaps of boredom. In fact, the one and only big happening in most of their lives is their death.

The postmaster drives up the hill to the bog in the postal truck while poor Willie peddles his bike back in the face of the driving rain. The family guides the postmaster to the digging and waits patiently while he examines the find. "What should be done?" they ask. Surely he would know.

However, as the postmaster quickly realizes, this box presents a number of problems. Who owns it? The township might claim it since it was found on common land. Then again, the Allan's might own it since they found it in their cutting area. Or again it might belong to the Island Council since they claim all items of antiquity for the common good.

The postmaster is also the constable. This box looks quite new. It could contain some loot from a robbery. In fact, St. John's Church had been robbed just the previous month, and this could be the items hidden for later disposal. The postmaster writes a summons for the church's pastor.

Again, in the driving rain, poor Willie is dispatched on his trusty bike to ride to the church with the summons. Willie hurries through the nave's entrance and, dripping wet on the church floor, excitedly waves the summons. The Evening Prayer meeting is just starting. The pastor reads the summons aloud, questions the boy, and excited by the possibility of recovering the relics, forgets the service and runs to the stable. He saddles the parish horse to ride to the bog leaving Willie behind to pedal his way back. The entire congregation, storm or no storm, turns at the church gate and follows on to the bog.

By this time the whole town is alerted, and in a wave of curiosity, they flock to the peat bog. Both the crowd and the storm are gathering for the event of the year. Behaving like true Scots, bets are placed, treasure or no, and the whole area begins to take on a festive atmosphere. The pastor, still robed for the service, the postmaster/constable in his uniform, men, women and children from the village, some dressed for the weather and others not, and, of course, the Allan's all gather around the box in anticipation.

The wind continues to gain momentum, and the rain strikes with such force that it stings the faces of those in the gathering. Those with umbrellas rather than rain gear find it hard to maintain their hold on the sail-like devices and are forced to close them to prevent disaster. This exposes them to the soaking torrent, but they stick it out, for this discovery is the highlight of their otherwise boring existence. "Open the box before we freeze to death," they murmur.

For the first few minutes after the pastor arrives, the question of ownership is debated. Finally, someone points out that little could be determined until the box is opened. "Open the box," the postmaster declares. A murmur of approval comes from the soggy crowd.

"Wait," says a voice from the rear of the pack. "We should get a picture of the opening moment for the paper. I'll get my camera." He hustles down the road to his croft to fetch his Agfa. Again time passes, and the storm turns nasty with bolts of lightening and gusts of wind bringing moans from the onlookers. Then the camera man is back, camera in hand and a tripod over his shoulder. The setup for the picture is complicated by the driving rain and the insistence for speed from the crowd whose voices can barely be heard above the roar of the wind, "Hurry, for the love of God!"

"Peterson should be here," someone shouts above the din. The schoolmaster is deemed the true 'brain' of the island. "He will know what the treasure is worth." Then more betting flies, based on the likely worth of the find.

"Forget him," someone responds. "We'll all be dead from lightening strike or pneumonia by the time he gets here."

Willie, who has just returned from his second trip to town, is exhausted and soaked to the skin, but no one takes pity. "Fetch the school master," his father commands. Pushing, rather than riding his bike against the wind, Willie makes a valiant start but stumbles to his knees in the mud as he swerves at a loud crack of the lightening.

"Never mind. I'll fetch him in the truck," yells the postmaster trying to be heard over the storm. Within minutes he comes back with the school master. The master had been walking on the road from town, coming to see the find.

In the mean time, the Allan's are busy arguing about how the fortune should be divided. The return of the postmaster with the school master shifts their interest back to the box. The chilling rain is beating down, and the howl of the wind is punctuated by flashes of lightning and crashes of thunder growing ever louder as the storm center arrives. The wind and rain will soon drive them back to their homes and warmth. It is now or never. As the two brothers attempt to lift the cover by hand, the nails resist, and they find themselves lifting the whole box from the peat. From the heft of it, it becomes clear that the box weighs well over one hundred pounds. This sets off a new round of betting with claims of the treasure's size enlarged to fit the heavy load.

Finally, the shovels are used as pry bars to lift off the lid. In 1770 the nails were all hand-made from iron slivers pounded to shape. The natural irregularities of the shanks make it difficult to remove the nails, and the box cover is locked in position as if the nails were screws. The brothers do not want to damage the box so the prying of the first corner is repeated around the perimeter as though they are opening a can of paint.

The roar of the wind, the crash of the thunder and the repeated flash of the lightening gives the whole incident the quality of the apocalypse!

The prying goes on inch by inch, but the lid seems to resist until a complete prying circuit is accomplished. Then, suddenly, as if in response to a particularly loud thunder clap, the whole cover springs free and falls to one side, exposing the body. The repeating flashes of lightning flood the area with strobe light. Millie is lying there with her eyes closed as if she had just fallen asleep, or perhaps better described, as looking like she had been buried just hours before, not centuries. The peat has preserved the box and its contents as no embalming could. There she lay with skin still pink, dark hair, which has continued to grow, filling the coffin, head twisted upwards and face contorted by the yank of the rope. To the onlooker's shock, the castoff she is attired in is a white wedding dress. Adding to the horror, the noose still hangs around her neck.

Rain pours into the coffin, matting the dress, the hair, and the noose against the body. Mud washes over the brink of the hole into the grave and dirty runoff forms rivulets like those of a volcanic eruption. A slurry of mud pours from the peat pile into the pressing crowd.

Lightning illuminates the scene as if a flash camera is snapping shots for the morning news. Thunder roars to a crescendo drumming out all conversation. The crowd closes in to get a better view of the monstrosity, those closest nearly falling into the box, only to be repelled in terror as the corpse suddenly sits bolt upright, eyes wide open, and screams over the howl of the wind and the crack of the lightning, "Why d'ya na leave me alone!"

CHAPTER ELEVEN

Kirkwall is the largest city on mainland Orkney. It was a royal burgh surrounded by a district called St Ola. St Ola is named for Olaf, the first Christian king of Norway. The city's name comes from the largest and oldest edifice, the Cathedral of St Magnus, (kirk), and its extensive walls.

The ruins of the Earl's and Bishop's palaces, and King's castle are ancient, but the cathedral is more striking in that it has been maintained in operating condition to this day. It was constructed in 1138 by Rognvald, Count of Orkney and dedicated to the memory of his uncle, Magnus who was the Earl of Orkney and was later canonized. Over the years the building has been kept in repair based on pew rents and public subscription.

Given the ancient nature of this city, the demise of the kelp, whaling, fishing and straw-plating industries plus the enormous collection of ancient monuments throughout the countryside, the direction of commerce is predestined, tourism. Yet, one can easily step back and imagine a time in history when commerce depended on the ancient cultivation of straw.

The Changeling

The Trows are one of the great mysteries of the islands. They are said to live comfortably in the bumps of land called howes that are so prevalent in the isles. They are not the misshapen mean, creatures of the Norwegians, the Trolls. They are not the magical creatures called the little people, the sheen, or the fairies reported by the Celts. Unlike these other creatures they seldom have commerce with humans with one exception, their children are often born sickly so they look for the opportunity to steal into a human newborn's home and make a swap.

The year eighteen hundred twenty one found the county of St. Ola and its royal burg of Kirkwall with approximately two thousand six hundred people facing the down turn of the kelp industry and, as you will see, on the verge of becoming the high fashion supplier for the Continent.

The east wind blew in across the bay, and the candles flickered inside their chimneys. The kerosene lamp on the rafter swayed ever so lightly from the breeze through the thatch. The moan of the wind broadcasting through the cracks in the window casings seemed to play a bass note to the colicky peedie (little) one's cries. "Wouldn't ya think she'd stop for breath," thought Millie, knowing the household's feeling about her new daughter.

"Coughed up her mother's milk again," Millie's father said removing the sour-smelling blanket from the cradle. "We should have watched the cradle, Hilda. I'll bet there is a muckle differ peedie person in the howe (barrow) out yonder."

"I don't want to hear such foolishness, Jock," Hilda scolded. "It is bad enough that she has a child out of wedlock. We don't want our neighbors thinking it's a changeling."

Jock was a lobsterman and owned his own boat. His son David and a brother-in-law were the crew. Owning a boat gave one standing in the community, and he had hoped to become an elder in the church. Little chance of that now. Fool headstrong girl getting mixed up with that Mickelson lad. Even though the lad in question had died before the wedding in a fishing accident, it still didn't make the pregnancy sinless. Abstinence was the rule, oft broken, but still the rule.

The sickly baby, was it God's punishment? Or was it a changeling, the offspring of a trow? A new infant was always guarded for the first night to prevent a felonious swap. Trow's babies were sickly, and so they were known to make an unannounced trade if the timing was right. None of Jock's family, including Millie herself, wanted this baby, so no one watched.

Millie named the child Mary hoping the mother of Jesus would accept the youngster as a god-child. Yet, on some evenings she would walk to the nearby howe and listen for child noises that would confirm a swap. The howe was always quiet.

So the child Mary grew, from a sickly baby, to a frail girl, to a skinny teen, but finally to a very short but robust woman. In time, the cold wind, damp weather and fickle lobster supply took the lives of her immediate family, and Mary was left alone in a village that questioned her humanity. She continued to live in her grandparents' house and made a living playing the man and continuing the lobster business. Her uncle still crewed, and Mary piloted the lobster boat from pot to pot. The astonishing thing was that she was unbelievably successful. Her pots were always productive, even when others were not. No woman could out-fish a man. There had to be some other explanation.

Kirkwall has a safe and commodious harbor which was in the process of being restructured to allow for the mooring of barques and loading facilities for grain, fish cured in the isles, cattle and other produce. At present, ships were held at some distance from the shore to clear the working area. Dories were used in the loading and unloading.

It was predawn when the barquentine entered the harbor. Only one passenger came in and drew a quiet mumble, "peedie folk," from the dock workers. His sea chest on end was taller than he was. A cart hauled the trunk up the hill from the waterfront on the village's only street. He drew more than his share of stares as he walked behind the porter. At the inn, they had to lower the register to have him sign in, but later in the day, the bank found his gold coin attractive and overlooked his dwarfish appearance.

Wattly Og was returning to the home of his parents after years of exile in Johannesburg, South Africa, where he had traded in gold from the Dutch mines. He seemed to have a talent for amassing golden wealth. As the Dutch government became aware of the profits from the knowledgeable speculation in the flow of gold from the mines, it took over the assay, purchase and distribution and enacted laws to shut down the speculators. So Wattly, fearing government confiscation, moved his bouillon into English banks and fled the country.

When he arrived in Orkney, he had no servants with him which disguised his true wealth. So the immediate attraction was revulsion to his stature.

You ask, "Who were Wattly's parents who had lived on Orkney?" Fair question, but I have no immediate answer. As it turns out, that is a very complicated question.

The kelp trade had supported the peasants of the island for generations, but those days were over. There was very limited agriculture on the island because of the lack of tillable land. The folk relied on money from wool, fish and other seafood, and animal husbandry including horses and cows. Of the parish's occupants, only a handful could be classified as "well off."

Wattly was a man of action, no matter what his appearance suggested, and must keep busy. Now I don't want to cast Wattly as greedily interested in accumulating obscene wealth. He was simply, by nature, an entrepreneur. Early his second morning, he set out on a walk to survey the opportunities. In less than a mile, his first commercial venture presented itself. A young urchin, not much smaller than Wattly, uninhibited by the caution of her elders, laughed at him as he strode by.

"What is so funny?" Wattly asked, already knowing the answer.

Without hesitation the whelp answered, "Ye 'er!"

"Is it my size?" he questioned.

"Ay."

"Is it my looks?"

"Ay," she answered again.

"Is it the way I walk?"

Again, "Ay."

"Do you like your hat?" Wattly then asked, looking at the straw bonnet crafted from native rye-straw.

She nodded, caught by his earnest stare.

"Who made it?"

"Me mither."

"And the one on your doll?"

"That bonnie one, too. De ye likes em ou noo?"

Without another word Wattly turned into the yard, mounted the stoop and knocked on the door. A woman of some thirty years answered. It was obvious that she had been watching from the window because she showed no concern at her caller's appearance. "Can I help you?"

"What would you charge for a bonnet as your daughter is wearing?" Wattly asked.

She hesitated several moments wondering if she should ask what he wanted it for, but finally decided to answer the question as asked. "One pence."

"Could I have one this afternoon?" he asked. So Wattly had his sample to send to London.

An order for one hundred at five shillings each came back that very next month, and an industry was born. (Before decimalization of British currency the pound was divided into twenty shillings and the shilling into twelve pence.) Now I know that you will scoff at this cottage trade, but within a few months it grew to the point that more than half the women of the parish were involved. As time went on, Wattly began to import Tuscan straw to supplement the native rye-straw for improved looks if not quality.

Once established, the hat trade took on a life of its own. Wattly hired a clerk, and he, in turn, hired hands to gather the hats, package them and ship them along with an invoice to the distributor in London. The hats were all the rage and now were finding their way onto the Continent. Other Orkney parishes such as Orphir began supplying the hats.

The women of Sandwick became especially adept at straw plaiting. This is no mean task for it requires a good deal of work. The fields are prepared by the men in the spring, including the manuring, and the seeds are sown thick so that the straw will be long and thin. In the summer the younger men cut the straw down before the grain ripens, tie it at the lower end into small bundles, and steep it in boiling water for an hour. Then they spread it on the ground to bleach in the sun. From there it is carted to the barn of the straw manufacturer. He pulls out the upper part between the highest joint and the grain, cuts it to the proper length, sorts it to the different degrees of fineness and then gathers it into bundles that are delivered to the houses of women who will plait it. The plaits are then regathered, washed, smoked, milled and, lastly, put into the hands of other women of Kirkwall, Orphir and St. Ola who sew them into bonnets.

The women of Kirkwall became used to the peedie man in their streets, and they even grew to respect him, dwarfishness and all. He was their hero. There were jobs to be had in the area at the distillery and the rope factory, but women were excluded from these places of gathering because it was thought that women belonged in the home. Those in public life were abhorred as tramps or harlots. Even gathering in private homes would have been unthinkable for "evil communications corrupt good manners," and "one sinner destroyeth much good." It was feared that the contaminated atmosphere would be destructive not only to their bodily health but also their moral health. The bonnets could be manufactured in the homes alone with the woman making as much as six pence a day. This was more than the men earned.

To many of us, as we look back at those times, the cottage industry of straw hats seems like a small thing, but to the islanders of that time, it was a boon. Imagine if you can, the condition of most families. They had few proper clothes, and animal skins were still worn. The black houses were mere hovels with center holes in the roof instead of chimneys for some of the smoke of the peat fire to escape. Most of the smoke lingered, irritating the eyes and lungs of the inhabitants and caking the roof and beams in soot that would gather until it fell back down on the inmates below. A second, approximately six foot square hole was cut in the roof at one end to be a window. In the middle of the one long room, cows, calves, pigs, geese and chickens shared the warmth of the peat fire with the family.

Oat and barley meal, milk, potatoes, kail, and fish were the main foods, but the amount often depended on the will of the landlord.

Wattly's heart was every bit as big as his stature was small. Not more than a week after he made his first trip to the area outside Kirkwall, he commissioned his clerk to consider the state of each family in parceling out the hat making. Later, he set up a school to teach the art so that those in need could receive remuneration. The gentry thought this odd for the church taught that the poor were so because they were sinners out of favor with God. Some months after he began this spreading of the wealth, the elders visited him to educate him in the need to support the landed instead of the evil, poor beasts that preyed on the land owners for food.

When it became obvious that he was intent on his ungodly method of reward, they then presented him a mandate. The tenants must pay a percentage, which some lords set as high as 50%, of their earnings, just as they had to give a portion of whatever they raised or grew on the land.

This was war as far as Wattly was concerned, and he was determined to win. Imagine the land owner's surprise when the bank stepped in and called the gentry's mortgages. It seemed that Wattly was now the bank's largest depositor.

In retaliation, they cast Wattly out of the church. However, this had no impact at all since he was not a member. When questioned about this, the pastor noted that it was the church's place to provide for the poor and not Mr. Og's. The church contributed a miserly ten pounds that year for their gift to the thousands of poor.

Some peasants could not make hats. There were twelve blind, seven insane, eight crippled and seven in jail for debts. Since the islanders had a basic revulsion for women working together in some form of manufacturing, a work house was out of the question. Considering the parish church's attitude, Wattly decided to fund an existing church of dissenters that had a building in Walls with the provision that they take in the blind, sick and homeless. The building was staffed at the expense of the hat trade, and the people of Walls were glad for employment as the nursing staff.

The rising fortunes of the peasants worried the landed gentry. It was already hurting them financially. Pay for servants had to be competitive with the hat earnings. In addition, the earned wages paid in coin to the renters made them less dependent on their lord. The slaves had become economically viable.

The landed gentry must get rid of Mr. Og.

Of course, none of the gentry wanted to be directly involved. No, the dirty work was to be left to others. The Wilsons would fit the bill. Angus Wilson had raised a brood of bad ones that were oft in jail and never in church. Willie Wilson was the brains of the group which just showed how impoverished they were. He could barely read. Yet, he was the only one in the family that could. Don't feel sorry for them. Their lack of righteous skills was more than offset by their rapaciousness.

One dark, cold night, disguised in black face and dressed in dark clothes, they broke in and pulled Wattly from his bed. Tied and gagged, he was placed in a large gunny sack and dragged to a cart which carried him to the seashore. There they threw him in.

Wattly struggled to free himself. The bad news is that the wind was offshore carrying him out some distance from his entry point. The good news is that the bag held appreciable air and floated. A lobster boat on a late return from the other side of the island, having lobstered off Graemsay, saw the sack bouncing about, pulled along side and skilled hands lifted the sack onto the deck as though it were a creel. Those hands belonged to Mary.

She was late that night because of that same offshore wind that blew the sack out to sea, but her night wasn't a loss. She had a hold packed with lobster, and after extracting Wattly from the sack, a fellow peedie person now warming beneath a woolen blanket.

The Wilsons were not so lucky. Apparently, several nights later, they were visited by a small army of peedie folk who seemed to come out of nowhere. It was said that the intruders sponsored a spirit of adventure in the Wilson family causing them to leave the island for places unknown.

While Wattly and Mary were busy discovering how much they had in common, the plotters were hatching another scheme. It was clear that they could no longer trust paid mercenaries. Yet, they could not risk an outright attack. They had to get Og to a place where they could deal with him without witness, a place they controlled. The distillery was the obvious choice. He distributed hats to the Continent. Why not whisky? Why, they would claim, if he could just see the unique process they had developed, he would understand the huge advantage he would have over ordinary whiskey.

Once in the door they could jump him, knock him unconscious, stuff him in a barrel and let him suffocate. Then they could ship his remains as cargo on a steamer to Calais or Copenhagen. Bodies were in demand for medical study on the Continent so they might well get more for the barrel's contents than for the usual barrel of whiskey. Of course, there would be some whiskey in the barrel to preserve the body and that could be an added sale item if it wasn't too contaminated with bodily fluids.

It was snowing when the committee arrived with the proposition for Wattly. They met with him at the ale house and shared a fine meal with their victim. Obviously, he was interested in their proposal. "Why, Mister Og, there would be no end to the potential. Everyone knows that our barley grain is the finest in all Scotland, but it is the process that marks the quality. The distillery is full of smoke from the fires now, but it will be clear this evening. We have plenty of lanterns to allow you to see our secret process. Just stop by at dark when the workmen have gone. We will be waiting."

They had him! After he left, they congratulated themselves and agreed to meet shortly before dark to be prepared for his arrival. They even left a tip for their very short waiter.

Unfortunately, from the owner's standpoint, the surprise party didn't go as they planned. Not one, but a dozen barrels were filled that evening. The peedie folk of Wilson's folly kept Wattly's appointment and made short work of the waiting gentry.

Now it was said that Wattly and his Mary left the island that same night before the constabulary could act. Yet, there was still a Mary living in the grandparent's house. She was not a peedie folk, but a full sized-woman. She was the spitting image of her mother Millie so no one questioned her claim. As for Wattly and the other Mary, when asked, the new Mary would look out over the moor to the great howe and smile.

(At this point I would like to answer your skepticism regarding straw hats made in Orkney. The Statistical Account of Scotland, Volume XV for 1845 notes in its chapter "General Observations on the County of Orkney," page 215, "The principle manufacture carried on, is that of straw-plait for ladies' bonnets: in which about 2000 girls are constantly employed, and almost all of our young women, and some of the married, do more or less, in the intervals of their other occupations." Later the report estimates that the sum received in 1833 from shipments of straw manufactured was L4800, a large sum in those days.)

CHAPTER TWELVE

SHETLAND

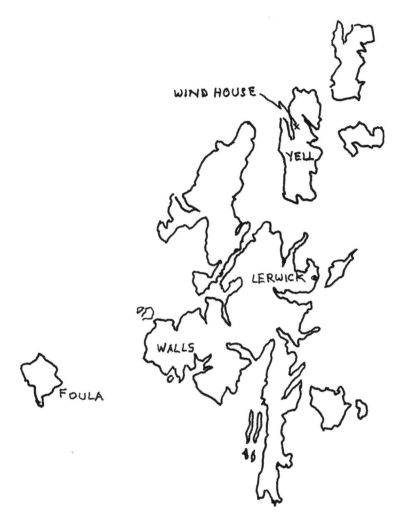

From Kirkwall in Orkney, I traveled north by ferry across the Norwegian Sea, to the latitude of Bergen, Norway, to the city of Lerwick on Mainland, Shetland, the largest of the Shetland isles.

These islands were in constant flux, being raided by Scottish pirates and retaken by Danes until King Harald established rule in 776. Gula Thing law was introduced by Hacon Adlestain. The center for this court of justice was Tingwall. (Later, when the court system came under the Scots, the court was moved to Scalloway.) Bishoprics were established in the isles, and parishes assigned. In 1271 Shetland was separated from Orkney and joined in union with the Faroes. The chief magistrate resided in Scalloway on Mainland Shetland. Finally, by a treaty in 1470 Shetland was reunited with Orkney and both were transferred to the crown of Scotland.

At the time of the transfer, the land was held by Udal tenure. This means it was handed down from father to son with no requirements that the offspring pay taxes or fees. The Scots made short work of this and seized the land. Scottish rule was so cruel that, time and again, the ruling parties, who ruled by grant from the crown, faced insurrection, and one after another had their grants revoked in order to restore peace. In 1600 the Earl, Patrick Stewart, built the castle that now stands as a ruin in Scalloway. Parliament, in response to grievances filed by islanders, revoked the Earldom and put Patrick to death for high treason. By the time of my travel most of the Norse families had either left or intermarried with the Scots. There were none of the original Danish landholdings left.

When I had traveled from the Western Isles to the Orkneys, the striking difference I noted was the shift from the rural and somewhat isolated communities with a Celtic heritage to a land of prehistoric monuments, mystical legends and Norse heritage. Now, the Shetlands brought me home. I could see New England in the quaint villages by the sea. Yes, there were still remains from the days of prehistoric man, but they were scattered and degraded. The Norse influence was even more pronounced with some Old Norse still spoken in family settings.

I looked forward to the planned excursions to the prehistoric village at Jarlshof and the Broch on the isle of Mousa. As you will see later, it was Jarlshof that pricked my imagination. But first, I needed to recover from a lost night's sleep on the ocean liner. I rented a car in Lerwick and headed for Walls to take a breather in my tour. Where Orkney seemed to be full of creatures of other worlds, this countryside, although barren, gave off a feeling of peace and contentment. I knew the stories would be different here.

Yet, it was a visitor, a tourist, who provided my first story, a man returning to the scene of the crime a decade after the events of the story. We sat on the glassed-in porch of the manor house overlooking Vaila Sound with a fair supply of wine and spent the evening reliving his odyssey. Listen to his story.

The Knitters of Walls

The world seems full of extremes. When things are going well, it's over-whelming, and when going badly, well, you know what I mean

I met Marjorie in her junior year at Northeastern. I was studying law and she accounting. I played hockey, and she was my one fan. She would watch and knit. Somehow she could knit without watching her hands. By the time we graduated, I had a drawer full of woolens and a bride. She was the love of my life, married on a shoestring and honeymooned in the park.

Marjorie got a job as an accountant for a wool merchant simply by showing him her knitting. I started out in a small law office handling insurance claims, wishing I were Perry Mason. The one thing we swore is that we would take that missed honeymoon as soon as we could afford it.

Both of my parents' families came from Mainland Shetland. My parents were first generation Americans. When they wanted to discuss something they wished to keep to themselves, they would simply switch to Old Norse, a language of Shetland forgotten in time. Out of self defense, my sister and I learned enough of the language to detect coming events. Not that my parents were harsh, they were both loving humans, and the language was simply something they shared in common. It was a part of their identity. They often talked of trips with my grandparents they had taken back to the island when they were children. They even had an album of old family pictures from their grandparents' time on the old farmsteads.

For her part, Marjorie had wanted to learn to make Fair Isle patterns, a task that required carrying four yarns at the same time on three needles. Since Fair Isle had only two hundred people on it, the knitting was actually done on Shetland using the wool from Shetland sheep.

So our honeymoon destination was to be Shetland, the old homesteads for me and the opportunity for knitting lessons for Marjorie.

Things couldn't be going better. By the end of the second year I was promoted to Junior Partner and Marjorie to Chief Accountant. We bought a small house and planned the trip for that summer before we would have children that could tie us down. No, there was no specific news in that direction, but we were working on it.

Then life changed. A small lump under my arm proved to be cancerous. Cancer was in my lymph nodes, and the tide of luck had begun to turn. Radiation treatments captured my energy and sucked flesh from my bones. Marjorie prayed for me every night and did everything she could to keep my spirits up. She was the one thing that kept me going. I struggled every day to work and keep life as normal as possible as the burning from radiation killed the cancerous cells and the good ones alike. Each day I counted the hours until I could be home with my wonderful wife.

Within two months after the end of the treatments, I began to feel more like myself, and we again talked of the trip to Shetland. The firm was willing to give me leave time for rest and recuperation. Marjorie had accumulated several weeks of paid vacation. Now was the time. We bought the tickets and made the reservations for our stay.

Just a few days before the departure, I found a new lump. One look at the doctor's face, and I could see he knew that the cancer was back. He told me to wait for the results of the biopsy before I considered treatment. I asked him what better treatment he had than the one already tried.

I told him I wanted to travel, and so I delayed the next appointment for nearly three weeks. He agreed. I could see he was in no rush, and I took that to mean he had no follow-on treatment. There was little more he could do.

But there was something I could do. I proposed to Marjorie that we go on the delayed honeymoon, that we enjoy it and each other. I insisted that we put aside the cancer and not even mention it the whole trip. Marjorie agreed, and we were on our way, first by jet to Prestwick and then train to Aberdeen. From there we took a ship ride on the P&O, some fifteen hours long, to Lerwick, Shetland. The rented car was waiting at the dock, and we were off to Walls, to stay at a lodge by the sea.

I was exhausted from the travel and spent most of the first day relaxing at the lodge. There was a conservatory with an ocean view where I could sit in a lawn chair and absorb the sunshine without the chill of the sea breeze. Marjorie became restless and took an afternoon walk. She returned in a little more than an hour with the news that a cottage industry not far away taught knitting as a sideline while knitting their product.

I felt rested enough to walk back with her to check out the opportunity. The hope was to arrange the lesson times so that they wouldn't conflict with other plans we had. We walked some half mile up the one lane road from the lodge to a small track off the road through the heather. There was a sign on a post at the start of the track noting *Knitting Lessons, Follow the Path,* so we followed the path over a hill and down to an ancient stone bridge crossing a brook. I told Marjorie there was probably a troll under it. It didn't seem to worry her. As we turned the side of the next hill, I saw a large, stone building with a huge, thatched roof. The front step was simply a large stone and the door, wood from some old sailing vessels still showing the ships' colors.

We knocked and then entered the building. Inside was one large room filled with women knitting. Suddenly, one cried out as if in pain. The others discarded their knitting and went to help her. Marjorie pointed out that it was simply a dropped stitch and could be easily fixed by undoing the row and starting over. We were both puzzled by the group's reaction. They all pitched in, getting in each other's way, helping the woman undo the row and restart the knitting. Finally, the woman nearest the door returned to her seat and, in a motherly voice, said how nice it was for Marjorie to have come back so soon.

She noted that each day's lesson would take about two hours and cost ten pounds. I asked her how many it would require, and Marjorie broke in noting that she had shown them her skill, and they had mutually agreed to ten lessons. I said, "For a total of one hundred pounds?"

The woman said, "No, ten pounds."

I noted that it would be twenty hours in all and at ten pounds total only one half pound per hour. That was a ridiculous wage. She should get ten times that, but the woman insisted. Rather than argue, I let it go realizing that I could always increase the payment later.

The next morning I took Marjorie to Upperdale, the Dale Burn, to the ruin of a farm that had once been my mother's family's leasehold. We shared a picnic lunch, and I told her some of the stories of the exploits of the Vikings my mother had learned from her father. Mid-afternoon we returned to the lodge, and Marjorie left for her lesson. I sat in the conservatory and fell asleep. At her return I was full of questions. "How did the lesson go? What were the women knitting? Why was there such a big deal made of a missed count the day before?"

Marjorie reported that the women were knitting squares that would be sewn together into a tapestry. They were doing this without a set pattern, working from their own experiences. She insisted that her attention was on the technique she was learning at the expense of observing the other knitters. Frankly, I couldn't picture a woven tapestry. What would give it the stiffness to keep it from sagging when it was hung? Perhaps it was some sort of covering I mused.

For the next several days we did research in Lerwick and field work, finally locating my father's parents' homestead. These were happy days for us, full of surprises and adventure. Each day we returned in time for the lesson. It was only fair that Marjory should get a chance to pursue her fancy as I did mine.

As the lessons continued, Marjorie seemed to get more interested, to the extent of practicing after class and discussing the new things she was attempting. Then, after about half the lessons were over, as if the sessions had changed to clandestine meetings, her reports stopped. Perhaps the change was in me, not Marjorie. As time wore on, I found myself considering the time left and thinking of the impending doom. I tried to hide this from Marjorie, but I'm sure she sensed the change and found it hard to discuss the good fortunes of her knitting lessons.

During the second week I was drawn to graveyards to compile a register of the deaths of each family member. Marjorie helped me take rubbings of special stones from the plots of the great- grandparents. I snapped pictures of the other plots of family members of interest.

The night before the last scheduled lesson, two days before we had to fly home, we had a celebration dinner to cap off our ten days of parole before the fateful return. Marjorie, always the one to restrict her liquor intake, let down her guard and became giddy. She talked of the things I could do with my life once we returned home; full partnership, a growing client base, perhaps sponsoring legislation in my field. I listened, but it cut like a knife. Wonderful dreams but, unfortunately, I was a walking dead man.

The next day I boxed all the research papers, rubbings and photos and mailed them back to the States so I wouldn't have to lug them back on the plane as excess baggage. I was late returning and expected to find Marjory waiting, but she was not there.

Her return from lessons had always been punctual. Since she didn't come back on time, I simply concluded it was some sort of celebration of her last lesson detaining her.

When dusk fell, I hurried down the road to look for her for fear she might have gotten lost. The sign was gone that had marked the path for lessons. In the dusky gloom I turned off the road through brush where I thought the path had been. Over the hill and down to the brook I struggled, wishing that I could locate the track and get out of the brush. At the brook I was surprised to find the ruin of a bridge. I surmised that it must be a much older structure than the bridge I was looking for.

First I thought to back track to the road but realized I didn't have time to start over before dark. So I rushed first up and then down the brook looking for either the path or the bridge. How had it become so overgrown? What had happened to the bridge? At least I could see the general direction of the house for the hill was still visible.

I waded across the creek and walked around the hill to where I believed I would find the stone building. Just as in the case of the bridge, I found a ruin. All that seemed to be left was a collection of stones.. The whole area looked as if it had been a hundred years since the last visitor. Where was Marjorie? Where was the stone building? I must be lost. She was probably waiting back at the inn saying, "Where is John?"

I hurried back to the inn, and not finding her there, I called the police. Waiting for them to come from Lerwick, I considered my story. I couldn't tell them the building disappeared. They would think I was crazy. I would have to tell them that her lessons were close by, but I didn't know where. That would force them to search the area.

Three constables and eight dogs scoured the area the next morning without finding a clue. Not too surprisingly their dogs traced Marjorie's progress to the area of the ruin, but there they lost her scent. They surmised that she was carried from that point to some waiting car or wagon. Whose car? She had no acquaintances in the area. Kidnapped?

They also found my footprints in the muddy bank at the ruin of the stone bridge. Had I followed her? They searched the hill and brook area for her body. Finding nothing, their attention turned to me. One constable asked if I had done something to get rid of her. I lost my temper and lashed out, striking the accuser. I was handcuffed and held until the Constable agreed that he had pressured me to get an admission of guilt.

Unfortunately, the owner of the lodge had seen Marjorie and me go out the first day to look over the knitting school which contradicted my testimony. I explained by stating I had only gone out to the road with her to get a general idea how far it was for her to walk each day. I disclosed my health condition, but I could see that they felt I was lying about not knowing the location of the lessons. I was then placed under house arrest in anticipation of the arrival of an Inspector Grant, a Chief Constable from Aberdeen.

Grant turned out to be a man in his sixties, tall, athletic in build, and aggressive in nature. In short, he was a bear. Rather than ask for my story, he attacked. "What did you do with the body?"

Who the hell was this irritating son of a bitch, I thought? "Do with the body! I'm trying to find her, and you are trying to pin murder on me."

"Do you expect me to believe this dumb story about your wife's going to school each day within walking distance without your knowing where. Show me the lumps from the cancer."

I took off my shirt and lifted my arm above my head.

"It looks like a simple growth to me. Who do you think you're fooling? Do you expect me to believe she left alone for her class yesterday! The owner saw you go out. We are going to plumb every sink hole in the area until we find her. Believe me, you make us sweat to find her body, and we will make you sweat in a cell once we locate her. Save us all a lot of time and yourself a lot of trouble. Tell us what you did with her."

"I loved her," I said lamely.

"Loved! Then you know she is dead. Where is she?" he demanded.

How could I tell a man like this about the building? It couldn't get any worse I reasoned so I agreed that I had lied. "You wouldn't believe the truth," I explained.

"Try me," he responded.

I retold the story from the beginning. I expected another harangue, but he only said, "As I guessed, another one. Four years ago I had a similar case not far from here."

"The same story?" I asked.

"Yes."

"Did you believe it?" I asked.

"No, but I do now."

"Did you find her?" I asked.

"No. Do you remember the tapestry? Well, there is an old folk tale about knitting the *tapestry of life*. Knitting the future so to speak."

"And these women are forced to do that?"

"Supposedly, they volunteer. It is their sacrifice to obtain control over the future."

"But Marjorie isn't a control freak. What would cause her to want to influence the future?" I asked.

"I think you know the answer to that better than I," he responded.

His words echoed in my ears as I left Shetland and flew home. "You know the answer." I did. The biopsy was non-malignant.

CHAPTER THIRTEEN

From Walls I traveled south through a storm to stay in Sandwick and visit Jarlshof, the remains of a Bronze Age village. But it was the guest house, the wide expanse of the sea and a storm that triggered my imagination.

The Little Blue Men

What you see is what you get

I had spent the day at the Quendale Mill and Jahlshof and returned to the guest house in Sandwick just in time for dinner. Mary Wren had organized an evening of entertainment for us. She had a fine voice and sang a cappella, folk songs of the Shetlands in the ancient tongue, Old Norse. After each verse she would translate and then, hardly missing a beat, sing on as if the song were continuous. She was a talented host if there ever was one. This night was a special one; Mary had agreed to tell us a story of the old days, a time between the wars, a tale from her own family and the primitive existence on Foula.

Mary's father had come from Orkney in a rather unusual manner. He had set sail in a small ketch on a bleak, December morning from Stromness, passing Graemsay and turning southeast in the direction of Scapa Flow. His planned route was to turn south to Mill Bay on the island of Hoy where he could pull out for the winter. His course was inner waterway all the way and in view of Hoy the full distance. This provided a barrier to shield him from the open sea. Then the fickle North Sea weather intervened to change his life.

About two in the afternoon, just as he breasted the headland with Cava dead ahead, the wind changed abruptly, and snow began to fall. Within minutes he found himself in a white-out, erasing all landmarks and requiring him to reef the sails and start the inboard. Line casts showed that the boat was moving with the wind in a northwesterly direction. He was moving back towards Graemsay. Between the rising wind and the tidal flow he guessed that he was drifting six kilometers an hour. He used the engine to keep the bow into the wind and rigged a storm sail. Then he cut the engine and tacked to beat into the wind and slow the northwest progress. The cold and snow formed a layer of ice on his oilskins, and the damp made him shiver. At any moment he imagined the high cliffs of Hoy looming at his stern reaching out like teeth to tear his boat apart.

Day turned into night, but the storm continued. He was exhausted, and as the waters calmed, he fell asleep. The rudder turned, the boat fell broadside, and the roll pitched him side to side in the captain's chair. Yet, he slept on. When he awoke, it was light, and the storm appeared to be past. Where was he? Had his drift remained in one direction? Surely, he was clear of the islands and well out to sea. All he had to do was set an easterly course, and eventually, if he could stay afloat, he would strike the shore of Norway. Conserving fuel, he set full sail.

Unfortunately, the sea wasn't through with him. The storm returned. Huge waves broke over the bow forcing him more north than east now. Again Mary's father set a storm sail to allow him to maneuver to ride the waves. The boat was shipping water, but he was afraid to run the pumps and use the last of his fuel. The deck was becoming coated with a slushy mix of sea water and snow. He knew in time this would form ice and chunks of it would move around like loose cannon balls. His time was running out. As the water in the bilge rose, the response to the storm sail slowed. As the boat climbed each swell, it would carve a path to the peak and then lurch forward and turn sideward as it fell down the back side. Then, for a moment, it was becalmed. In that interval it had to be forced back into the wind to face the next wave. That recovery was getting slower as the boat became waterlogged. If it didn't come about, the oncoming water wall would strike the boat sideways and roll it over. Down it would go under kilotons of hydraulic pressure; chances are, never to rise again.

He could not feel his feet, and his hands were like iron mittens. It was time to face the end bravely. He had put up a good fight. What more could he do? He was freezing to death. Then, dead north, the western cliffs of a huge island appeared through the storm. As he drew nearer, it became apparent that the eastern shore was lower then the steep western side. If he could swing further to the east, he would tack into the island's shore and ride the swell until he could abandon the boat. He noted a light house ahead. Once past the light he would be running north on the east shore. He would have to set the main sail, tack and come about fast, or he would simply blow past the island.

He was at the mercy of the wind. It now appeared that the boat would hit the light. Then the wind shifted. Like some great hand, it pushed him east of the light up along the eastern shore and finally along a small bay. The wind shift saved him from striking the lighthouse but prevented him from tacking under sail.

He reefed the storm sail and started the motor. He gave the boat full throttle to the west, beating against the wind, and driving him shoreward. Then he remembered that he had a good six feet of keel draft. He would ground well away from the shore, and be swept sideways into the rocky shoals that formed the northern edge of the bay. The swell was coming in at eight feet, and there was clear indication of undertow. The boat would not survive, and he would drown in the icy water. He put on a life jacket and launched the emergency rubber life raft. He crawled out of the cockpit and onto the raft, and pushing free from the doomed sailboat, attached the oars. His hands felt like wood, and he struggled to grip the oars.

Someone was on the shore waving to him.

At first the raft began to drift back out to sea passing the sailboat, but his rowing brought him back in, riding a frothing breaker. Next, undertow sucked him back out before he had the chance to jump to safety. Another breaker brought him in close enough to grab a rope, tossed by the person on the beach. Pulling on the rope, he battled the outward water flow. He swept in with the next breaker, actually touching the sand of the beach. This time he jumped and was surprised to find himself unable to stand on his frozen feet. The shore person grabbed him and dragged him to safety.

Mary's father passed out from exhaustion.

The bed rolled and tossed and turned as though it were navigating a huge sea all by itself. He reached out to grab the edge and came away with a handful of rye-straw. That fistful of straw somehow seemed to stop the motion. He found himself in a makeshift bed by a peat fire in a cottage. There was an old woman staring blankly at him as if he were furniture.

"Seanachar, is he awake?" a voice asked. A younger woman walked into his line of vision and knelt beside the bed. "How do you feel?" she asked.

"Water," Mary's father replied.

She poured something into a cup and said, "Warm tea." She pressed it to his lips, and he swallowed.

He hurt in so many places he couldn't count them all. The most painful were his feet, so painful that he wished they were removed. Then a troublesome thought hit him. What if they had been cut off? He looked down expecting to see no feet and was relieved to see the bulge in the bed covering. When he looked under the covers, he found that his feet were there but horribly chapped.

"I'm Myra, and this is my grandmother," the young woman announced. "This is our home."

It turned out to be a marvelous place to recuperate. My father tried walking on the third day with remarkable success. His feet and hands both peeled as if they had been sunburned, but the damage was minor considering the exposure.

It was obvious that the young woman was overjoyed to have his company in her bleak life. She spent hours talking with him each day as he gained strength.

Myra's mother and father were dead but had left a legacy that, although small, was enough to assure the two of them, her and her grandmother, of the essentials to survive in their island existence. Originally, the family was from the Isle of Lewis, and this explained the Gaelic name for grandmother. Myra's father bought the farm when she was a child, and so her home had been this island. Both father and mother were drowned in a ferry accident in Orkney on their way to visit his family, who were owners of a fish exporting business that eventually became the basis for the legacy. The grandmother had a stroke when she learned of their deaths and had been quiet ever since.

With Myra's patient care, Mary's father grew stronger day by day. Within a month he was able to accompany them on their weekly journey to Walls on the ferry boat to buy provisions. Myra waited on her grandmother and was a slave to her mental condition. On the boat it was obvious that she was determined to be beside her to be sure she was safe and to humor her as she spoke to what Myra called "the little blue men."

Automobiles and wagons were boarded first and foot passengers last. Moments after the last passenger came across the gang plank, the ferry was underway. The boat kept a strict schedule. As they pulled out, Seanachar made her way quickly to the aft rail. Once there she waved to the bubbles in the wake calling them by name. "Hello, Charlie. Hello, Jock. Hello, Johnny."

Myra humored her by joining in, and eventually, Mary's father also played his part calling out, "Jock, is that you? Charles, you look pale; nice to see you again."

And then the quiet grandmother began to talk to her little blue men, "Wait until you hear what we are going to do today." It was as if her tongue were loosened by their presence. She kept up the one-way conversation for a full half-hour until the old dame grew tired and had to be helped to a deck chair.

Poor Myra, she was putting up with this foolishness just to humor her crazy, old grandmother. He had fallen in love with Myra and was quite sure she felt the same for him. So he stayed on with her even after his health improved, paying board to help out and spending time with grandmother to give Myra a break.

Each weekend the madness was again played out as they sailed to and from the mainland, talking to the little blue men the grandmother seemed to feel were just like family. Charlie, Jock and Johnny kept her company in the wake all the way to the docking at Walls, and she felt required to recognize them and pass the time of day. Myra and he joined in, but he often grew tired of the charade and thanked heaven that it was only on boat trips. The rest of the time at the farm she was quiet and non-responsive.

He asked Myra who these people were she saw, and she shrugged. Obviously, she was glad to see her grandmother respond to something, and it gave her a chance to have a conversation with her, such as it was. Otherwise, the silence of the old dame would grow on your nerves just as if she talked a blue streak.

Mary's father and Myra were soon living as if married, but Myra would not make it formal as long as her grandmother lived. She explained that it would not be fair to him to tie him down to caring for an invalid woman. However, it was a blessing having him around, and he was welcome to stay on as long as he was willing to put up with the old lady's quirks.

As luck would have it, Myra soon became pregnant, and the old dame died about the same time. Mary's father was anxious to make things right as soon as possible, so he again proposed marriage, and she welcomed it. He talked of his fine estate in Orkney, and she agreed to move there as soon as she could make arrangements to sell the old farm.

It was the first weekend in June and a fine day for a trip. They would travel to Walls for a civil ceremony. She dressed in a beautiful summer dress she had bought for the occasion and he in a suit with a hat that dared the wind to blow it off. They were both in high spirits. They planned to list the farm for sale that very same day with a realtor in Walls. After the wedding they would spend a week in Lerwick on honeymoon. Then, she would return to the farm to get it ready to sell while he would return to Orkney to make preparations for their future together.

The boat for the mainland left at noon, and they had set the marriage appointment for mid-afternoon. It was a beautiful day with a blue sky and hardly a cloud. They boarded the boat hand-in-hand. They were free to live their lives together, happily ever after.

As they were pulling out, Myra released her grip on his hand and pulled away. She ran to the aft rail. Waving, she called to the trailing wake, "Hello, Charlie. Hello, Jock. Hello, Johnny. Wait 'til I tell you what we plan to do today."

CHAPTER FOURTEEN

I felt it was time to move to a more northern residence as a base to visit the northern isles of the chain. The new location was still on Mainland but north and west in Hillswick, Northmaven. The family I stayed with spoke Old Norse as their first language but shifted to Scots English in speaking to me. It amazed me to see how easily they did this, and the Scots English had, at least to my untrained ear, no Norse accent.

Very early one day I drove to Toft to ferry to Ulsta on Yell. My objective was to explore Muness Castle on the northern most island of the Shetlands, Unst. To get there I had to drive the length of the island of Yell and ferry again across to Unst at Gutcher. I was in a hurry, and Yell was just property to be traversed. Rounding an uphill turn, Windhouse, a towering ruin on the hill to my left stopped me cold. I could not pass it by.

It was only later, after I had taken its picture and finished my trip to Unst that I learned the gruesome details of this haunted place.

The local library folklore collection traced the house back to the 1400's when it was built on what some said was a prehistoric graveyard. The house was evil from the start and finally torn down, and stone by stone, rebuilt down hill from its original foundation. Unfortunately, the evil followed, and the house was deserted in the early 1900's to become the ruin I saw.

Stories of haunts and skeletal findings at Windhouse abounded, but the one that caught my imagination was the one about the visit of a trow at Christmas. It was that visit which lead to my story.

MacFarland is Dead

Long Live MacFarland!

In the islands, life centers on the sea. Everywhere you go, the sound of gulls can be heard. Boats from the smallest dinghies to the open Orkney skiffs are moored in every bay and used by the true Shetlanders to provide fish for meals and sale. There is a scattering of power and sailing boats owned by visiting tourists. Still others are available for charter, skippered by enterprising islanders.

I hired a skippered sailboat at Toft to sail up Yell Sound and, if possible, into Whalefirthvoe to take a picture of Windhouse from the water. The skipper, a young lad named Jamie MacFarland was in the process of re-claiming his birthright. His first acquisition was the very boat we were sailing on which had once been the property of his great-grandfather, James MacFarland. It was a ketch rigging rather than the yawl rigging common in the area. His great-grandfather had sailed it across the Atlantic from New England to Scotland and eventually to Yell where it was wrecked. Jamie explained that while one person could sail the boat, an overseas trip would require another hand taking shifts at the tiller. MacFarland's reluctant wife had been pressed into service in much the same way seamen of old were acquired to sail on merchantmen.

"Why a picture of Windhouse from the sea? You can see it from the road. If you walk up the drive to the fence, there is an excellent shot of it silhouetted against the sky. It makes an imposing picture." Of course, Jamie was right, and I had already shot it from the front. I explained that I was writing a story about a recorded incident of a visit to Windhouse by a trow that had come up from the voe. I needed a picture from the voe in the direction of the house,

As we cleared the docking area and sailed across to the Yell shoreline, Jamie continued the conversation. "Do you write stories or rehash old fairy tales?"

"Stories," I answered.

"I like stories myself. Fairy tales are for children. Say, would you like to hear a true story my mother told me? This boat is in it."

"Can I retell it?"

"You paid for the charter; you can have the story as a kicker." Jamie settled back and lit his pipe.

"My great-grandfather James MacFarland had been a big shot for the railroad. He had led an active life, and retirement wasn't going to stop that. He was a man's man. He had been all over the empire expanding rail lines and establishing service. He was a bull of a man and commanded respect both by his large stature and by his achievements. Yet, like us all he had grown older and was now retired. He had bad knees and so walking was not enjoyable. There were no airplanes or autos in those days so land trips were beyond his capability. He wanted to continue adventuring. He wanted to sail. The move here to the island, with access to both the North and Norwegian Seas, was his choice.

My great-grandmother Mary MacFarland was a different type of person. She was society. To her this was the end of the earth.

The people on Yell at that time were either fishermen or farmers or both. The women were hard workers and provided cheap labor. The missus had help with the house work, and he had crew for his sailing. She, on the other hand, suffered due to the moist climate, from acute arthritis. She longed for the drier climate of Edinburgh."

From the polish of the story, it was obvious Jamie had told it many times. Was this tale part of his service?

"In those times," he continued, "the cure for arthritis was considered to be the royal touch. Here in Yell there was no hope for a royal presence, but a substitute was known. A few crowns and half crowns of the first Charles had been carefully handed down from father to son and were considered effectual throughout Shetland. Through all the counties in Shetland there were those that had been "cured by the coin." Unfortunately, the missus wasn't going to be one of them.

On the south side of the island there are two good harbors of Burravoe and Hamnavoe, about a mile distant from one another, but on the west side, about eight miles to the northward, the shore becomes high and dangerous. From West Sandwick to Gloup, the northern most point on the island, there are only two places for a distance of eleven miles where a boat can be moored, Whalefirthvoe and the Dale of Lumbister.

It was a tacksman of Robert Bruce of Burravoe, one of only two principle resident landlords at the time, who found the wreck. It was MacFarland's sailboat battered by storm and partly sunk. It had washed up on a small sand spit between rocky abutments of Yell Sound, mast broken, sail gone and the punt missing from its deck attachment. Had MacFarland drowned or escaped in the punt?

After several months it was felt reasonable to declare that MacFarland was dead. A formal memorial service was held in the parish kirk of Mid Yell. Although the people of the island were a clannish group not adopting outsiders easily, they had found MacFarland to be a good sailor, a fair fisherman and a source of income for services rendered. Since most of the parishioners of the kirk lived within four miles of the kirk, the turnout was generous. The widow was shown the kindness of the parish in the form of attention and companionship. This was undeserved on her part since she had shown no compassion for her neighbors in their times of need."

Here Jamie stopped to change tack up along the island of Bigga turning off the course that would have landed us in Ulsta, the ferry port. Then he returned to his history.

"With the issue of the death reported, the railroad sent an agent to make arrangements for the payment of the life insurance given as a perk to all top management. It was not worth a fortune but was double indemnity for accidental death which, in this case, amounted to some five thousand pounds.

It was mid-summer when the rail man, Bertrum Hale, arrived. He was a tall, gaunt man in his early sixties. He had come by coach from Lerwick and was clearly exhausted. He leaned on his cane in the doorway, and for a moment, the Missus thought he would fall over. "Missus Mary MacFarland?"

"Yes?"

She couldn't help feeling that this stranger was sick for his eyes were filled with tears, and his jaw fell open showing a lack of teeth. "I'm Bertrum Hale from British Rail to..cough,cough, investigate the .. cough, death insurance claim. May I ..cough, come in?"

He followed her into the kitchen where she offered him a seat at the table with his back to the fire. He sat and instantly seemed to fall asleep. She asked the servant to put tea on and left him there while the water heated. In those days it wasn't unusual for travelers to go without sleep for days bouncing along in coaches over unimproved roads and over voes in barge-like ferries. Finally, the servants helped him to bed to recuperate. Missus could care less. She had the necessary papers from the priest, witnesses to the finding of the wreck and the lengthy waiting period to substantiate McFarland's death. Her factor was already looking for a residence in Edinburgh for her, and she was looking for someone to buy the Yell house."

Again the story had to wait for a correction in our heading. We had just passed the island of Uynarey and, with a correction to the north, were sailing close to the shore of West Yell. Jamie asked me to hold the tiller on course for a few moments while he went below. I have to say my sailing experience was a bit limited and the feel of the wheel foreign to my grip. We were not that far off shore. For the moment I forgot the story line and with clenched teeth I held the tiller and prayed. Jamie returned with a coffee mug for each of us. It was a wonderfully clear, sunny day, and the wind was light and firm. Yet, in the Shetlands the temperature, nearly always moderate, was slightly on the cool side. I accepted the coffee gladly, first to give back the tiller, but also to provide a warming sensation to offset the ever-cool ambient. Jamie started again as though he had never stopped without the usual, "Where was I?"

"Finally, they both sat in the kitchen and went over the documents. Bertrum, the rail man, agreed that they were in order but felt that without a body there would have to be an inquest to settle the issue of the cause of the death. That same afternoon, Bertrum traveled by shay to the cottage of the tacksman who had found the wreck. He then went with him to examine the remains at the shore. "The punt is gone you say?"

The man was cautious and didn't want to draw attention for he had his position to consider. "Probably torn loose by the storm."

The rail man knew the reason for the punt. "When he skulled out to the mooring, wouldn't he have left the punt on the buoy? Why was it aboard in the first place?"

"Don't know, but it wasn't at the mooring, so he must have had it aboard. Widow said he usually did. It weren't at the wreck."

"Could he have used the punt to put ashore in the storm?"

"Not likely. If the storm did all that damage to the ketch, the punt wouldn't have lasted a minute. Especially without the drough. It is still on the deck of the ketch."

Here Jamie stopped to explain that the drough was a sea anchor, a hoop with a conical sock of canvass attached which, when thrown overboard, would drag in the water. Tied to the bow of the boat it would keep it pointed into the storm. The punt could then face into the wind and perhaps ride out the storm waves. Of course, its first use would have been to save the ketch itself. Little good it did still packed on the deck. Had it been used, MacFarland might not have needed the punt at all.

"Where would the punt end up if it didn't wreck on the shore?" asked Bertrum.

"Next stop is the Faroes on the way to Iceland."

"It is? Well now."

Arrangements were made, and over the next few days, the wreck was hauled in for further inspection. In the interim the rail man questioned neighbors, reviewed the weather conditions at the time of the accident and sent dispatches to Lerwick.

The Marconi telegraph system of that time required that the decoded messages received in Lerwick be carried by post to their destination. This delayed the messages by at least a week and also made each message public knowledge. There were no secrets."

Jamie stopped to replenish his pipe.

"Then a message originating in the Faroes arrived in Lerwick for the widow. The details spread through out the islands like a lightening bolt racing the actual hard copy to the isle of Yell. "*MacFarland here, very ill, stop. Will make arrangements for ship to Norway hospital, stop. Please advise wife in Zetland on Yell. Full stop.*" It was not dated.

The widow was shocked to say the least. Rather than a cry for joy, she read and reread the message saying, "Can't be. Can't be." Bertrum left for Lerwick. Within the week a second telegram arrived, "*James MacFarland has died aboard ship before reaching Norway. Full stop.*"

Mary MacFarland simply collapsed.

With that the railroad insurance man returned to Yell to inform the onagain off-again widow that an inquest was required to produce a death certificate. The widow and her solicitor must come to Lerwick for the hearing.

When the inquest was held in Lerwick, the widow and Bertrum Hale presented the evidence to date, and MacFarland was declared legally dead."

Jamie stopped the story here and pointed to the cliff-strewn coastline backed by the hills of West Yell. "Mean place to be caught in a storm." One could see cottages along the path of the highway far above the cliff line, but it was obvious that there was no safe landing area. In fact, ahead the cottages petered out as we sighted the Head of Brough. Beyond that the shore was desolate.

Again Jamie went on.

"The very next day a telegram arrived at the MacFarland solicitors, *"Error in ship contact, stop. MacFarland is alive in Norway. Full stop."* The inquest was hastily reopened, and the death finding reversed. The widow was visibly shaken."

"How could it get so messed up?" I asked Jamie.

"One way is for the ship to shore message to be garbled. That wasn't telegraph as we know it. That was the era of noise transmission of Morse code. Transmitters were very weak, and messages had to be relayed from ship to ship. Many times the same message would arrive several times by different routes and be somewhat changed depending on the number of relays and the fist or sending capability of the various radio men along the way."

Jamie took up the story again. "Three weeks later a telegram arrived at the house in Yell, *"Sailing in the morning on St Olaf for Lerwick, stop. James. Full stop."* It was just a matter of time, and MacFarland would be home.

Yet in the time it took the telegram to make it to Yell, the Lerwick papers were reporting, "**St Olaf lost at sea. All aboard presumed drowned.**"

The rail agent traveled from Lerwick to Yell to bring the news of the tragic sinking. It again took him several days to regain his strength. He noted that another inquest would have to be called and made arrangements for the widow and her solicitor to be in Lerwick in two weeks. Yet, unbelievably, before he could leave to return to Lerwick yet another telegram arrived. *"Rescued by steamer 'Bern' of Suisse registry, stop. Am in Lerwick and will be home shortly after this telegram arrives, stop. James. Full stop."*

"No. No. No!" The widow repeated in frustration as she went to her room in obvious distress. She waited there for low tide late that night. Quietly she crept down the hall to a utility closet. There she took a rag and tied it around a short broom handle. She soaked the rag from a bottle of lamp oil. Holding it in front of her to keep the oil from dripping on her clothes she went out the back door. She walked swiftly to a ledge that formed a walkway along the cliff. This ledge ended in a path which lead down to the stony beach. As she reached tide level, she ducked under an overhang, normally under water, and into a hidden cave exposed at low tide. She lit the oil-soaked rag and climbed above the tide line to a rock shelf. There she examined the overturned punt. It was still in place. She raised it to look at the murdered man's decomposed body she had hidden beneath it. She lowered the makeshift torch to light the horror's face. "MacFarland is dead! Dead! Dead!" she screamed.

"So he is," said Bertrum Hale from the cave's entrance.

CHAPTER FIFTEEN

Why do I roam these isles? Of course, they are chock full of mysteries. But that is true for much of the world. The fact is I enjoy them. I feel at home in them. They are my roots.

As I noted earlier, my mother is Florence Catherine MacLean, of the Mac-Leans of Point Prim, Prince Edward Island.

As the family on PEI grew in number, several of them emigrated to the United States, settling in a city that had an industry that appealed to Scottish men, quarrying. My grandfather owned a stone shed. Quincy granite, an especially hard and beautiful form of granite, was prized above others for large buildings. The Scottish emigrants owned the pits and stone sheds and the Italian emigrants operated them. An interesting note is that the competing quarries in Barre, Vermont were just the opposite with the Italians owning and the Scots operating.

Combining imagination and history the following comes to mind:

From prehistoric times, the Scots have been quarry men. On Orkney, ancient monuments such as the Stones of Stenness, the Ring of Brodgar and Maes Howe date back over five thousand years. There is no end of quarried standing stones throughout the Western Isles. This is just the tip of the iceberg. There are stone brochs, duns, castles and finally buildings dotting the landscape. Then there are all the churches, statues, grave stones, fence posts and markers. In some cities, even the streets and sidewalks are cut granite. It is only fitting that at least one story address this major Scottish occupation.

The Quarry

A hole is to dig

First, you strip off the topsoil. Next, comes the hardpan. Finally, you have the base stone, granite. At the start, the hole is no more than one hundred feet in diameter, and for the first twenty feet in depth, dry. Holes are drilled at intervals in the granite, packed with explosive, topped with blasting caps. Wire is run to a hand plunger some hundred feet away. The warning is given, "Fire in the hole." Everything stops. For ten seconds it is deathly quiet. Count them! One, two, three, four, five, six, seven, eight, nine, ten. **Blam**, the stone parts, granite dust spews into the air, and an irregular slab is broken free.

Straps are placed, the hook attached, and the slab lifted by the crane, "eek... eek...eek," to the rim of the hole. From there it is hauled to the stone shed where a large saw squares the surfaces, "zip...zip...zip."

Once the pit is deeper than twenty feet, seepage occurs, and a pump is added to pump out the excess water, "swoosh, swoosh, swoosh."

Granite is a very hard stone. It was cut into brick-sized chunks and used as paving stone. However, a granite roadway can be rough, and sometimes bumpy, and so granite was finally replaced by asphalt as the preferred paving material.

Granite is a beautiful stone. It comes speckled in red, pink, gray or black. In early times it commanded a huge premium as the preferred builder's stone. It exuded permanence and for this quality, was the mainstay for constructing banks and funeral homes. With the advent of structural steel, granite was replaced by concrete as the preferred building material.

Granite takes a fine, glossy polish and can be carved by sand blasting into practically any shape with or without an inscription. People were dying in increasing numbers. This market for tombstones would never go away.

"Swoosh, swoosh, swoosh, eek...eek...eek, zip...zip...zip, There is fire in the hole!" (quiet, one two three....ten) **Blam**, hundreds of tons of cut and polished stone were produced each day.

"Swoosh, swoosh, swoosh, eek...eek...eek, zip...zip...zip," the hole grew deeper, and as it did, a second pump had to be added.

"Swoosh, swoosh, swoosh, swoosh, swoosh, swoosh, eek...eek...eek, zip... zip...zip," the hole went deeper still until the boss man said, "seventy feet." That is the depth the crane can lift. That is the depth the boss man set as the goal. And so digging was stopped.

"Swoosh, swoosh, swoosh, swoosh, swoosh, swoosh, eek...eek...eek, zip... zip...zip. There is fire in the hole!" (Quiet, one, two, three.......ten) **Blam!**

After a year or so, first the drillers, then the cutters and finally others in the hole, began to cough. The silicone dust would take its toll. Silicosis was the verdict.

"Swoosh, swoosh, swoosh, swoosh, swoosh, swoosh, eek...eek...eek, zip... zip...zip. There is fire in the hole!" (Quiet, one, two, three.......ten) **Blam!**

Now there is a place where the coughing workers finally go. A place where their work is immortalized. To get there you pass through a break in the quarried granite stone wall and under a gate that says it all. "**Ye who enter this broad gate come never too early nor never too late.**"

Now that the hole was at maximum depth, the slabs were cut out of the side, and it grew in diameter. Each day you would notice a new worker or two and realize where the old ones went. Would they run out of workers or stone first?

It was easier to break slabs free from the wall than from the bottom so production increased. The boss man was pleased, especially on the day they produced five hundred tons, and he remarked, "Well, bless my soul!" He would get a bonus.

"Swoosh, swoosh, swoosh, swoosh, swoosh, swoosh, eek...eek...eek, zip... zip...zip. There is fire in the hole!" (Quiet, one, two, three.......ten) **Blam!**

And as the hole grew wider, a third pump was added. "Swoosh, swoosh, swoosh, swoosh, swoosh, swoosh, swoosh, swoosh, swoosh, eek...eek...eek, zip...zip...zip."

Eventually the hole consumed all the saleable granite, the supply of workmen was depleted, and the graveyard full. The pumps were shut off, the crane dismantled, and the stone shed burned to the ground.

And when all in this world is done, and the angel Gabriel arrives at the Scots while reading the final role, I know he will be interrupted by sounds from the past.

"Swoosh, swoosh, swoosh, swoosh, swoosh, swoosh, swoosh, swoosh, swoosh, eek...eek...eek, zip...zip...zip. There is fire in the hole!" (Quiet, one, two, three.......ten) **Blam!**

ABOUT THE AUTHOR

John Edward Radcliffe is a Wisconsin story teller who both writes and tells stories based on his travels to remote places throughout the world. He was born in 1937 and brought up on the south shore of Massachusetts so he developed a love of the open sea. He has a BSEE from Northeastern University and a MSE from Rensselaer Polytechnic Institute. John has traveled and worked in Europe, Asia and Africa. His Scottish Isles family background and his romance with the sea made the isles his favorite biking, exploring, and story hunting grounds.

20315195R00096

Made in the USA
San Bernardino, CA
06 April 2015